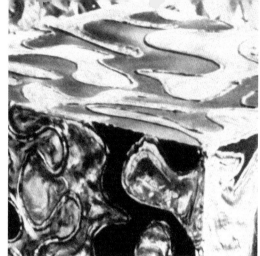
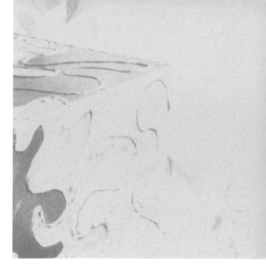

Paul Evans
Designer & Sculptor

Jeffrey Head

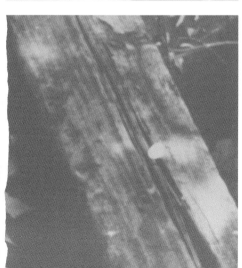

Schiffer
Publishing Ltd

4880 Lower Valley Road • Atglen, PA 19310

Cover and interiors designed by John P. Cheek
Type set in Modern No. 20/Gill Sans Std/Adobe Garamond Pro

ISBN: 978-0-7643-4166-3
Printed in China

Schiffer Books are available at special discounts for bulk purchases for sales promotions or premiums. Special editions, including personalized covers, corporate imprints, and excerpts can be created in large quantities for special needs. For more information contact the publisher:

Published by Schiffer Publishing Ltd.
4880 Lower Valley Road
Atglen, PA 19310
Phone: (610) 593-1777; Fax: (610) 593-2002
E-mail: Info@schifferbooks.com

For the largest selection of fine reference books on this and related subjects, please visit our website at
www.schifferbooks.com
We are always looking for people to write books on new and related subjects. If you have an idea for a book, please contact us at proposals@schifferbooks.com

This book may be purchased from the publisher.
Please try your bookstore first.
You may write for a free catalog.

In Europe, Schiffer books are distributed by
Bushwood Books
6 Marksbury Ave.
Kew Gardens
Surrey TW9 4JF England
Phone: 44 (0) 20 8392 8585; Fax: 44 (0) 20 8392 9876
E-mail: info@bushwoodbooks.co.uk
Website: www.bushwoodbooks.co.uk

Contents

Foreword

Paul Evans was a protagonist of the mid-century American craft-based art and design movement that spread across the United States after World War II. During his life, he became one of the leading American craftsman-designers and his work often challenged traditional boundaries between craft and furniture design.

Today, Evans's designs still defy simplistic stylistic descriptions. A table of welded steel and slate from the mid-1960s resembles Oscar Niemeyer's hyperboloid structures in Brasilia. The ironwork on a room screen Evans crafted out of black walnut and 22-karat gold leaf in the mid-1950s is reminiscent of Jean Royere's undulated metalwork. The glamorous *Cityscape* series designed for the manufacturer Directional, sheathed in a sleek patchwork of metal, mirror, and wood, evokes the luxury of Eileen Gray's geometric, gold and silver plated screens. Then, unexpectedly, one stumbles upon the *Corrugates*, dining chairs made in 1976 of corrugated cardboard and burlap. Could these chairs have been Evans's homage to the *arte povera* movement in Italy during the 1960s? Are they Evans's simpler take on Frank Gehry's corrugated cardboard *Wiggle Chair* made in 1972? These questions shall remain unanswered.

Paul Evans's designs pose a challenge that will forever remain unconquered: categorization. Slick and shiny one moment; rough and sculptural the next. Seductive and sophisticated one second, intimidating and perplexing the next. Evans's furniture presents no homogeneous narrative. Instead, like a jealous suitor, each piece demands singular, devoted attention. Perhaps the only thing Evans's designs share in common is their panache and presence.

The period immediately after World War II was characterized by burgeoning economic prosperity and mass production. The 1950s was a material decade. After years of doing without, Americans were finally able to buy cars, houses, furniture, clothes, and such luxuries as dishwashers, television sets, and stereos. However, Paul Evans's handmade objects offered a humanizing counterpoint to the postwar machine aesthetic.

Despite the record levels of consumption that characterized the United States after the war, it is important to highlight that contemporary furniture designers like Paul Evans faced a slow, uphill struggle in which admiration was often displayed by a small number of adventurous cognoscenti. When Evans began working as a designer, living rooms of American suburban homes were mostly filled with unremarkable assortments of furniture in pseudo-historical styles made in Grand Rapids. Conformity was the rule of the game. As a result, Evans's professional success, in the United States and abroad, represents multiple victories. Namely, the triumph of craft over mass-production, daring over revivalism, and recognition of the beauty of handcrafted furniture.

Crafter of welded metal furniture and designer to the stars, Paul Evans's furniture found homes in the collections of individuals such as Prince Binder Fisal of Saudi Arabia and Mrs. Vanderbilt Webb. Yet, while we have access to images of his furniture and lists of his noteworthy clients, few pictures exist today of his full-scale, residential commissions. As a result, we are left wondering what his interiors looked like, such as the 1979 commission at 2 Sutton Place that involved the redecoration of an entire apartment. Evans created a world we can only know through words: gold, raw silk walls alternating with beige, gold acrylic ceilings, all with recessed lighting, built-in cabinetry, suede upholstered seating, and chrome accents. In the tradition of Jacques-Emile Ruhlman's Grand Salon in the *Hotel d'un Collectionneur* at the Paris 1925 Exhibition, Evans's interiors were luxurious and sumptuous, their furnishings expensive and evidence of a commitment to craftsmanship. This book allows a glimpse at what this great American designer created and invites us to fantasize about the special projects we shall never see.

— Adriana Kertzer

Preface

The furniture designed by Paul Evans (1931-1987) remains the most unusual, functional, and expressive work of the mid- to late 20th Century. Although his furniture is readily identified, it is not easily categorized nor does it have the features usually attributed to modernism. Among his peers, which included Harry Bertoia, Charles Eames, George Nelson, Sam Maloof, George Nakashima, Wendell Castle, and many others, he was considered an innovative craftsman and artist with an unconventional aesthetic. Now, almost fifty years since he first began designing, his work still represents contemporary, modern design, independent of a particular era. Although one could perceive the work as futuristic forms of bas-relief or baroque.

Evans's work is virtually free of historical reference. Influences are unknown, non-existent. Although he was aware of the work of his peers and past generations of furniture-makers, he did not seek to interpret or re-work their designs. In an effort to try to understand Evans's work, many have described it as brutal. This is misleading since there is no parallel between his furniture and brutalist architecture. While Evans's furniture is dramatic, it does not share in the reductivist, invariably patterned and unadorned designs of brutalism.

Using the techniques and materials of a sculptor, Evans created hundreds of furniture variations, each with a highly textured, distinctive look. He made a full range of cabinets, tables, chairs, beds, and other furnishings from metals like aluminum, bronze, chrome, silver, and steel, sometimes with gold-plating. At other times he mixed materials, combining walnut burls or leather with metal to produce rich, touchable surfaces. If he designed a dining table and chairs, there was naturally a sideboard, but Evans typically went further and created a suite of matching platters, candlestick holders, ashtrays, and other accessories. Nothing was too large or too small to design. Competitors and peers were always curious about his techniques, since there was very little evidence for how something was made. This quality added to the furniture's appeal and continually resulted in strong sales. Although his furniture was in production and could be ordered from a catalog or showroom floor, each piece had the characteristics of a one-of-a-kind, made-to-order piece.

During his lifetime Evans saw the exhibition of his work in many museums and galleries, including the Museum of Modern Art (MoMA) in New York. Currently several Evans pieces are on permanent display at the James A. Michener Art Museum in Pennsylvania in the museum's exhibition, Intelligent Design: Highlights of Arts and Crafts and Studio Craft Movements. The museum is also preparing for an extensive, full-career retrospective of Evans's work. In the fall of 2011, the Museum of Arts and Design (MAD) in New York included Evans in their exhibition, Crafting Modernism: Midcentury American Art and Design. Additionally, exhibitions in Paris, France and Milan, Italy are introducing Evans's work to an international audience looking beyond the widely recognized, iconic designers of the 20th Century.

Introduction

Paul Evans's professional and personal qualities were inseparable. As a Quaker, he believed in treating people well, being honest, and doing a good day's work. He was an even-tempered, light-hearted, caring person, who gave people the opportunity to develop their own skills.

When he arrived at the factory in the morning he would socialize with every employee, every day. Once at his desk, Evans would draw and doodle his ideas, introducing a new set of designs to work on, making each day different and interesting.

For Evans, designing was an evolutionary, trial and error, hands-on process that he directed and refined. He enjoyed experimenting, but, if a design did not work, it did not bother him. Instead, he would try something else or start again. Evans found the stress and pressure of the design business thrilling and energizing, and actively sought it out.

This dynamic attitude also made socializing with him an entertaining activity. Summertime backyard parties at his home always led to everyone ending up in the pool with their clothes on, including Evans.

Evans made the annual Christmas party an event, coming up with amusing ways to give out bonuses. One year he blew up balloons, placed rolled up money inside and attached the balloons to a board. Different colored balloons represented different amounts. Each person had a turn firing a nail gun at a balloon and kept what they shot.

Evans enjoyed socializing, and people were a source of inspiration to him. He was very family-oriented and treated all his employees like family. When the pressure was on, Evans motivated people in an exhilarating and exasperating ways, helping them recognize their own talents and challenging them.

While artistic development was Evans domain, he was open and flexible about letting other craftsmen influence the design of completed pieces.

— Dorsey Reading

Paul Evans and Dorsey Reading at work on a copper loop panel. 1962. *Courtesy of Dorsey Reading.*

Paul Evans was raised in a Quaker home. He was born in 1931 and named after his father, Paul Robert Evans. After graduating from Wagner Junior High School in Philadelphia, he attended the George School Preparatory, a Quaker school in Newtown, Pennsylvania, where his father taught English and served as the Head of the English Department for many years.

Evans's mother, Trina A. Evans, a painter, taught him to paint and encouraged his artistic interests. Prior to entering the senior high school program in 1947, Evans studied with painter Jack Follensby of New Hope, Pennsylvania. However, once he started at George School, Evans's major courses were in woodworking and design.

When he graduated in 1949 he briefly attended the Philadelphia Textile School (later Philadelphia University). Evans did not like the school. His casual watercolors were not in the style of the program so he left and started an apprenticeship with his uncle, Ed Truett, a metal smith in Belleville, New Jersey. Evans credits his uncle for providing him with a foundation in metalsmithing, leading to Evans applying to The School for American Craftsman.

The School for American Craftsman (RIT)

Evans attended The School for American Craftsman at the Rochester Institute of Technology (RIT) from 1950 to 1952. He received a full academic scholarship from arts and crafts patron, Aileen Vanderbilt Webb who supported Evans, encouraging his development as a young artist and, later, as a professional designer. She continually recognized his talent and helped introduce his work to a larger audience. Evans acknowledged Webb's influence throughout his career.

Evans 1952 class picture. Rochester Institute of Technology. *Courtesy Archives and Special Collections, Wallace Library, Rochester Institute of Technology*

On the first day of school, Evans met classmate Elaine Bebarfald. The two of them were racing for space on an open workbench in the metal shop and ended up sharing an adjoining workbench. Evans and Bebarfald were the only students in their freshman class to complete the Metalcrafts Program. As a student Evans was active in the Student Council and a member of the RIT wrestling team, where he was sometimes known as "Bruzzy."

The Metalcraft Program was a curriculum based on an apprentice system. Twenty-eight hours of each week were devoted to technical development in the workshop, seven hours each week were set aside for art and design, and five hours a week for academic subjects and design. This total of 40 hours a week made for a challenging schedule, with classes meeting from 8 A.M. to 5 P.M., Monday through Friday.

For his metal studies, Evans worked under John Prip and Lawrence Copeland. His instructor for art and design courses was Fred Meyer. All were well-regarded, exhibited craftsmen and designers.

Evans received training in copper, brass, bronze, and silver. He learned to raise hollow-ware, forge flatware, do sand casting, and to enamel with copper and silver. He also studied jewelry design. The workshop environment gave Evans the opportunity to do practical experiments. He worked with various materials and dealt with design issues related to production and marketing. He received his highest grades in Metal "Technics" and Marketing, and progressively improved his grades in art and design. Knowing that he wanted to set up his own silversmithing shop after completing his program at The School for American Craftsman, Evans realized he needed to continue his formal studies. "I have much more to learn and problems to solve…to work out freer and better forms in hollowware and flatware," he wrote in a letter from school.

Evans silver container completed as a student. 1952. *Courtesy Archives and Special Collections, Wallace Library, Rochester Institute of Technology*

While finishing his Associate in Applied Science Degree (AAS) in metal craft from The School of American Craftsman (RIT), Evans was invited by the Scholarship Committee at Cranbrook Academy of Art in Bloomfield Hills, Michigan, to compete for a one-year scholarship. In his application he wrote, "Metalwork has been one of the neglected areas in American design, and has been unfortunate in being controlled by traditionalists in its design, and by the taste of large scale commercial producers who have demonstrated little interest in contemporary form." He also indicated that he wanted "to experiment with some of the forgotten methods such as niello and inlays." (Niello is a decorative engraving technique for metal.)

Competing against 1200 applicants, Cranbrook awarded Evans the Ellen S. Booth Memorial Scholarship for Jewelry and Metalsmithing. This was a prestigious award, since Ellen Booth and her husband, George, were the founders of Cranbrook.

When Evans started at Cranbrook in the fall of 1952, he and Bebarfald had married earlier in the year and were living in Sturbridge Village. She had given birth to their first son, Paul Evans III, known as Ricky. She and Ricky stayed behind while Evans attended Cranbrook. His class schedule was metalsmithing, Monday through Friday from 9 a.m. to 4:30 p.m. His instructor, Richard Thomas, remarked that Evans's ability was "excellent mechanically" and encouraged Evans to expand his experimental approach. However, in the middle of the spring term of 1953, Evans was offered a position in Sturbridge Village, Massachusetts, and, wanting to return to his young family, left Cranbrook before completing his scholarship.

Paul "Bruzzy" Evans (in white cap), 1952, on the wrestling team at Rochester Institute of Technology. *Courtesy Archives and Special Collections, Wallace Library, Rochester Institute of Technology*

Silver bowl, c. 1952, by Evans classmate Elaine Bebarfald, who later became his wife. *Courtesy Archives and Special Collections, Wallace Library, Rochester Institute of Technology*

Sturbridge Village

Sturbridge Village is a re-created rural New England town in Worcester County, Massachusetts. It is a "living museum" and gives visitors an experience of what life was like in the 1830s. It includes demonstrations by traditional craftsmen who create and sell reproductions, and make repairs. In the early 1950s, its craftsmen also filled requests. For example, if a visitor wanted a Duncan Phyfe style table it was made in the woodshop. In addition to traditional crafts, at that time, the Village offered contemporary designs. In 1953 Evans was hired as the resident contemporary silversmith at Sturbridge, although he was still expected to make traditional designs. He made silver bowls, cups, flatware, and jewelry,

and offered custom services to visitors. He was successful at Sturbridge and his work sold well, although he felt the constraints of marketing and profitability of silversmithing. Sturbridge was not creative or expressive enough for him, so he began thinking about decorative objects and furniture design. In 1955 Sturbridge Village decided to stop offering contemporary crafts, so Evans and other craftsmen started to look for work. The search became more urgent and occurred even more rapidly when a severe storm brought forceful winds and heavy rains causing dams to break in Sturbridge and other nearby areas. Flooding wiped out roads, houses, and bridges and briefly changed the local economy.

■ Footed bowl with salt and pepper shakers, c. 1952. Sterling silver. 3.25" x 6" (bowl). *Courtesy of Wright.*

■ Pitcher, c. 1952. Pewter with rosewood. 11" x 5". *Courtesy of Rago Arts and Auction Center.*

■ Candlesticks, c. 1952. Pewter. Approximately 14" x 2". Circa 1952. *Courtesy of Wright.*

Lambertville and New Hope

The Evans family initially moved to Lambertville, New Jersey, across the Delaware River from New Hope, Pennsylvania, in 1955 immediately after the Sturbridge Village floods. That same year, when the Evans's second son, Keith, was born, the family moved to New Hope

Evans was already considering the move to New Hope prior to the flooding and talked with New Hope wood craftsman Phillip Lloyd Powell about working in the area and collaborating. Powell had a successful showroom, where he sold the lamps he designed with walnut. Powell also offered the Eames plywood chair and the Hardoy "Butterfly" chair, which both sold well. During his days as a student at The School for American Craftsman, when Evans visited his parents who lived in the area, he often stopped in Powell's showroom. It was there that Evans saw first-hand the marketing opportunities for modern design. The two craftsmen developed a friendship, which started with Powell selling the bronze bowls Evans was making in school.

In 1956, Evans and Powell started collaborating on different pieces, which combined their respective crafts of metal and wood. In addition to furniture, the two men completed various commissions for clients who enjoyed the complimentary design of their work. Although each craftsman maintained his own workshop, they formed Designer's Inc., and had the designs produced by a local manufacturer. The line paired mahogany or walnut and pewter. Pieces were typically marked with an engraved round metal label, "Designers Inc. Paul Evans." A charger, a whiskey bottle, candlesticks, a cutting board, and several types of salt and pepper shakers were part of the line. Designer's Inc. was specifically made for distribution by Raymor and was a successful line for the company. Many of the designs were sold through the Lord & Taylor department stores. Evans's first contact with Raymor took place when he was a student.

Irving Richards, one of the partners of Richards Morganthal, founder of Raymor, often visited The School for American Craftsman to see student work. Several years later in 1955 that contact led to Evans designing menorahs for Raymor, which sold through Macy's other department stores. The menorahs were done with turned brass candleholders and a brass star of David. There were five types of bases, all made with black walnut, each one named after a glorious brother from a Hebrew story. Evans was responsible for the design but not involved with production. In 1966-1967 he also designed six prototype clocks for Raymor. These were done in a welded steel, starburst pattern. The clock faces did not have numbers. The hour and minute hands were gold leafed without a second hand.

Evans and Powell learned from each other, worked together, and shared clients until 1966. At that time Powell felt he was stopping Evans from growing the business. Powell wanted to keep the business small. When the two men stopped collaborating, they remained friends and continued to admire each other's work.

Another significant association for Evans was with Dorsey Reading, which was far-reaching and vital to Evans's long-term success. In 1959 Evans visited the local high school in Lambertville asking the industrial arts teacher if any students were doing metal work. The teacher recommended Reading. Later that year, after graduating, Reading went to work for Evans and stayed with him 23 years.

Reading's career with Evans started out with washing the landscape pebbles that covered the floor of the showroom Evans and Powell shared. From those early days of not saying no to Evans, Reading's position evolved into foreman. This increasingly important role helped Evans maintain an experimental approach. Reading became largely responsible for the development and prototyping of products based on Evans's sketches on onion skin paper.

■ Paul Evans and Phillip
Lloyd Powell showroom
(1955-1964). South Main
Street and Waterloo Street,
New Hope, Pennsylvania.
Courtesy of Dorsey Reading.

■ Paul Evans and Phillip
Lloyd Powell showroom,
with window painted for
the holidays by Powell.
1960. South Main Street
and Waterloo Street,
New Hope, Pennsylvania.
Courtesy of Dorsey Reading.

Paul Evans steel sculpture in Paul Evans and Phillip Lloyd Powell showroom. Dimensions unknown. 1960. South Main Street and Waterloo Street, New Hope, Pennsylvania. *Courtesy of Dorsey Reading.*

NO. **20** SOUTH MAIN NEW HOPE, PA. PHONE 2440

- PAUL EVANS • METAL
- GIFTS / IMPORTS • FURNITURE / ACCESSORIES
- PHILLIP LLOYD POWELL • WOOD

Paul Evans and Phillip Lloyd Powell showroom card. Date unknown. New Hope, Pennsylvania. *Courtesy of Dorsey Reading.*

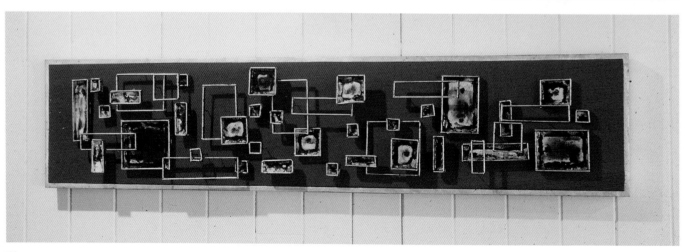

Paul Evans metal wall sculpture in Paul Evans and Phillip Lloyd Powell showroom. Dimensions and date unknown. South Main Street and Waterloo Street, New Hope, Pennsylvania. *Courtesy of Dorsey Reading.*

Salt and pepper shakers, 1956–1957. Paul Evans and Phillip Lloyd Powell for Designer's Inc. Walnut with pewter inlay. Larger: 4" x 1.75" x 1.75". *Courtesy of Rago Arts and Auction Center.*

Ashtray, 1956–1957. Paul Evans and Phillip Lloyd Powell for Designer's Inc. Walnut with pewter inlay. 2" x 3". *Courtesy of Rago Arts and Auction Center.*

■ Candlesticks, 1956–1957. Paul Evans and Phillip Lloyd Powell for Designer's Inc. Walnut with pewter inlay. 13.5" x 3". *Courtesy of Rago Arts and Auction Center.*

Container, 1956–1957. Paul Evans and Phillip Lloyd Powell with Jens Risom for Designer's Inc. Mahogany with pewter inlay. 4" x 3". *Courtesy of Rago Arts and Auction Center.*

Salt and pepper shakers, 1956–1957. Paul Evans and Phillip Lloyd Powell for Designer's Inc. Walnut with pewter inlay. Larger: 4.5" x 3.25" x 1.25". *Courtesy of Rago Arts and Auction Center.*

Table lighter, 1956–1957. Paul Evans and Phillip Lloyd Powell for Designer's Inc. Walnut with pewter inlay. 6" x 2.5". *Courtesy of Rago Arts and Auction Center.*

■ Charger, 1956–1957. Paul Evans and Phillip Lloyd Powell for Designer's Inc. Mahogany with pewter inlay. 17.25" diameter. *Courtesy of Wright.*

■ Low table, 1956–1957. Paul Evans and Phillip Lloyd Powell for Designer's Inc. Walnut with pewter inlay. Dimensions unknown. *Courtesy of Dorsey Reading.*

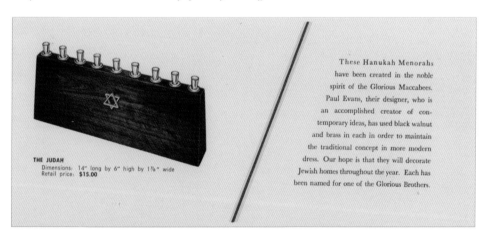

THE JUDAH
Dimensions: 14" long by 6" high by 1⅞" wide
Retail price: $15.00

These Hanukah Menorahs have been created in the noble spirit of the Glorious Maccabees. Paul Evans, their designer, who is an accomplished creator of contemporary ideas, has used black walnut and brass in each in order to maintain the traditional concept in more modern dress. Our hope is that they will decorate Jewish homes throughout the year. Each has been named for one of the Glorious Brothers.

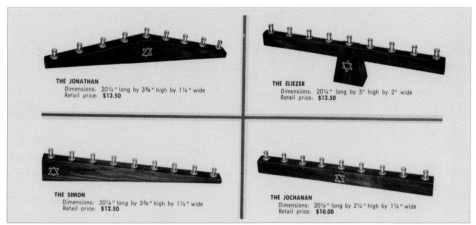

THE JONATHAN
Dimensions: 20¼" long by 3⅜" high by 1¼" wide
Retail price: $13.50

THE ELIEZER
Dimensions: 20¼" long by 5" high by 2" wide
Retail price: $13.50

THE SIMON
Dimensions: 20¼" long by 3⅜" high by 1¼" wide
Retail price: $12.50

THE JOCHANAN
Dimensions: 20¼" long by 2¼" high by 1¼" wide
Retail price: $10.00

■ Brochure for menorahs designed Paul Evans for Raymor, 1955. *Courtesy of Dorsey Reading.*

■ Lamp, 1956. Paul Evans and Phillip Lloyd Powell. Walnut, stainless steel, linen shade. 30.5" (height). *Courtesy of Wright.*

■ Storage unit, 1963. Paul Evans and Phillip Lloyd Powell. Welded and patinated steel with sliding door cabinet and interior light. Walnut shelves and natural cleft slate top. Gold leaf patchwork. Approximately 8'.4" x 10'.10" x 20.5". *Courtesy of Rago Arts and Auction Center.*

■ Wall-mounted cabinet, 2005. Paul Evans and Phillip Lloyd Powell. Walnut, iron with gold leaf. 18.50" x 8" x 48.75". *Courtesy of Wright.*

■ Picture frame, c. 1970. Patchwork design. Paul Evans and Phillip Lloyd Powell. Silver and gold leaf on lacquered plywood, walnut and glass. 20" x 38" x 5". *Courtesy of Wright.*

■ Wall-mounted cabinet, c. 1960. Paul Evans and Phillip Lloyd Powell. American black walnut, iron with 22k gold leaf. 57.75" x 10.25" x 23". *Courtesy of Wright.*

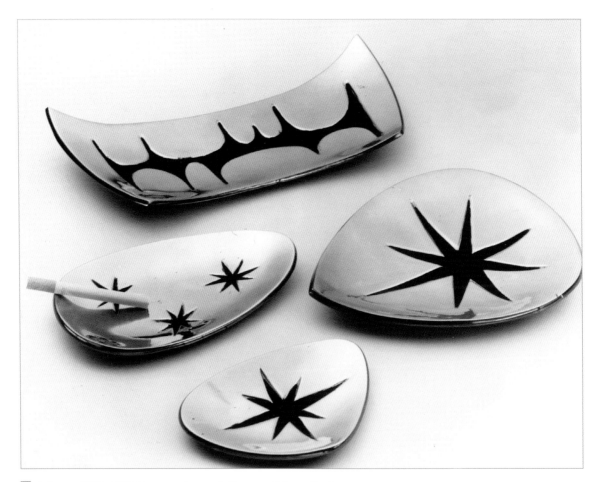

■ Ashtrays, 1956–1957. Pewter and enamel. *Courtesy of Dorsey Reading.*

■ Plates, 1956–1957. Brass and enamel. *Courtesy of Dorsey Reading.*

■ Vases, 1956–1957. Steel and enamel. *Courtesy of Dorsey Reading.*

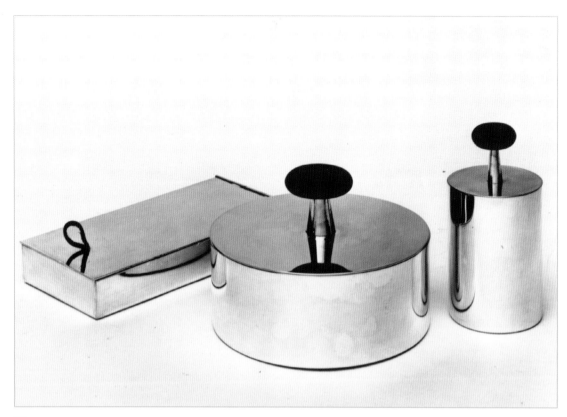

■ Containers, 1956–1957. Brass and rose wood. 1956–1957. *Courtesy of Dorsey Reading.*

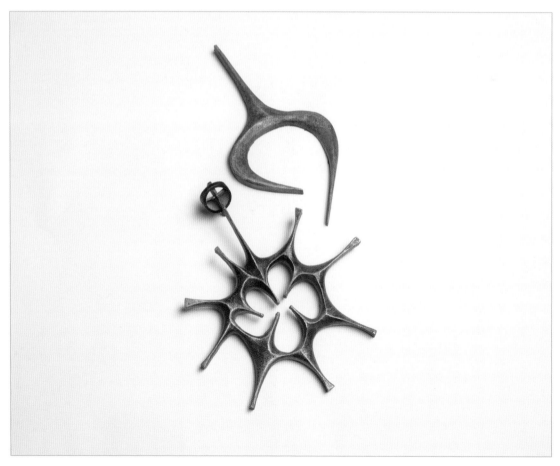

■ Door knocker for Directional, 1956. Cast in bronze and aluminum. 10" x 9.5". *Courtesy of Wright.*

America House

Paul Evans first started showing his work at America House in 1952, when it was located on East 52nd Street, before it moved to its last location across from the Museum of Modern Art on 53rd Street in Manhattan.

America House was a venue for craftsmen to exhibit and sell their work. For some, it was their only forum. America House offered high quality handmade objects by artist-craftsmen from all over the country. It started in 1940 and, before it closed in 1971, did more than any other commercial outlet to create a lasting appreciation and market for handcrafted designs.

Aileen Vanderbilt Webb who started America House was already familiar with Evans from his attendance at The School for American Craftsman, a program she sponsored as part of her life-long effort to support and promote handmade crafts. Webb was also the founder of The American Craft Council in 1943. While he was still a student at The School for American Craftsman in 1952, Evans

submitted his silver and rosewood coffeepot to the annual summer competition held at America House. The competition was "open to young Americans thirty years of age and younger who designed and executed their own pieces." Evans was 21 years old, and won first prize in metal, as determined by a panel of judges that included Edgar Kaufmann, Jr., of the Museum of Modern Art, Furniture Designer Edward Wormley, and Gallery owner Bertha Schaefer, among others. Evans's coffeepot was displayed in the second floor exhibition area along with salad servers, which earned him a certificate from the judges.

Evans as a student with examples of his work, for a Rochester Institute of Technology program brochure, 1952. *Courtesy Archives and Special Collections, Wallace Library, Rochester Institute of Technology.*

In 1954, Evans had a more formal showing of his work at America House, which featured silver and pewter pieces. It was a shared exhibition with furniture designer Loren Manbeck. Evans and Manbeck, during this time, were studio craftsmen in Sturbridge Village and worked in the same building creating contemporary objects, contrasting the reproductions generally made in the Village. Manbeck also attended The School for American Craftsman, although two years before Evans, and studied woodworking and furniture design.

For the exhibition, Evans showed treated pewter pieces that did not get marred by water such as a bowl, a punch set (with 24 cups), a two-handled pot, a coffee service, candlesticks, a tea caddy, and a box. The sterling silver pieces were flatware (a place setting for 7) with ebony handles, salt and pepper shakers, salad servers, a bowl with a saw-toothed edge at the rim, a four-piece coffee service, a tea strainer with an ebony handle, and an hors d'oeuvres spear. Prices in the exhibition ranged from $10 for a pewter bowl to $700 for the silver and rosewood coffee service. Many of the pieces sold during the exhibition.

Evans's next show at America House was in 1961. This time he shared the exhibition with fellow New Hope designer Phillip Lloyd Powell. Between Evans and Powell, they showed more than 30 wood and metal pieces. Some were collaborative pieces, and others were individual designs. Many were prototypes. Evans's and Powell's idea of presenting prototypes was to generate custom orders, which turned out to be an effective, long-term marketing approach for both designers. America House helped ensure the success of the designs by offering a service to clients to facilitate custom orders.

The show included a sculptured steel wall divider measuring 15' x 100'. This was a very early piece in the *Sculpted Steel Series*. It had a variety of in-laid, smaller metal fragments and patterns, painted in different colors and patinas. One of the tables Evans and Powell collaborated on had a travertine top with a strip of walnut wrapped along the edge. The table was set on a series of gold leafed vertical rods. Aileen Webb had a version of the table with a slate top in her home in Shelburne, Vermont, and had Evans's tables from the show in her Upper East Side penthouse apartment. A variation of the dining table was shown with metal arches. Different sized coffee and side tables were also available. The table base options were walnut, copper, or iron. Some had an oxidized finish.

At the time, Evans described oxidation, the acid technique that created the textured patterns in the metal, as "...burning other metals on it like icing a cake." He also remarked, "that handmade products should show the hand. Good line is not enough because that can be produced industrially" and that "furniture should have detail and richness..."

Detail. Wall-mounted stereo cabinet. Patinated sculpted steel door. *Courtesy of Rago Arts and Auction Center.*

Wall-mounted stereo cabinet, date unknown. Interior shelves, four sliding doors, and one hinged door with patinated sculpted steel. Paul Evans and Phillip Lloyd. Walnut with pewter inlay. 14.5" x 66" x 19.75". *Courtesy of Rago Arts and Auction Center.*

Between 1961 and 1965 Evans's work appeared in the America House catalogs and on several occasions was featured on the cover. The catalogs were a small representation of what was available and made it possible for people outside of the area to make purchases. Other craftsmen showing work along side Evans were Peter Voulkos, Franz Wildenhain, and Thomas Stearns. Evans did a range of designs for America House, from sculpted steel front cabinets to bronze ashtrays. Evans metal boxes were a popular item. They were made of pewter, bronze, and copper with the largest size 16" long, 8" wide, and 6.25" high. Sculpted steel pieces such as a wall relief were also available and could be "ordered to specifications" if a customer did not want the 24" x 36" design shown in the catalog.

His relationship with the America House was important in introducing him to the New York decorative arts and furniture market. Through America House he gained the attention of the public and the industry. His craft was widely seen and his ability to offer custom made studio pieces created a unique alternative to standard, production work from traditional manufacturers. The starting point for the Paul Evans "look" was initiated and to a large extent identified through America House. When Evans's relationship with America House ended in 1966, it understandably had more to do with Evans wanting to reach an even wider market for his designs.

Sculpted panel detail, c. 1965. Welded and patinated steel. *Courtesy of Dorsey Reading.*

Sculpted panel, 1965. Welded and patinated steel. 30.25" x 3.25" d x 30". *Courtesy of Wright.*

Detail. Sculpted front hanging wall cabinet, c. 1965. *Courtesy of Wright.*

American House catalog, c. 1965.
Courtesy of Dorsey Reading.

the finest in American crafts

america house

Paul Evans Studio

Many of the designs Evans created for the America House evolved into more elaborate studio pieces. Decorative sculpted steel panels became room dividers and door fronts for cabinets. This further established the Evans studio, as requests for sculpted steel pieces continued throughout the 1960s. Each sculpted piece was hand-forged, labor-intensive, and specially designed. Euclidian shapes, star forms, and various patterns become motifs. Set in a grid-like arrangement, the panels became a rich, intricate collage of metal, color, and technique. For these, Evans used patinated steel with enamel, bronze, brass, and gold leaf. Approximately seventy-five cabinets with sculpted steel panels were made. Optionally, many of the cabinets could be wall-hung or placed on a base.

Wavy front cabinets with their stylized and abbreviated "S" curves, first introduced in 1966 and also made during this time, were in contrast to the divided arrangement of the sculpted steel panels. The sense of movement and depth is another example of Evans's ability to think three-dimensionally.

Rather than produce in a limited range of scale, Evans created monumentally sized pieces and small, hand-held pieces like ashtrays or boxes. The dramatic nature of the work was not compromised by the size of an object. For buyers with different budgets, this approach also made it possible to acquire a variety of complementary pieces.

Paul Evans (l), Dorsey Reading (upper right) and Cool (Robert Lee Thomas – bottom right), c. 1966. *Courtesy of Dorsey Reading.*

■ Asymmetrical sculpted panel, 1970.
Welded and enameled steel with gold
leaf. 25" x 24" x 3". *Courtesy of Wright.*

■ Detail. Asymmetrical sculpted
panel, 1970. *Courtesy of Wright.*

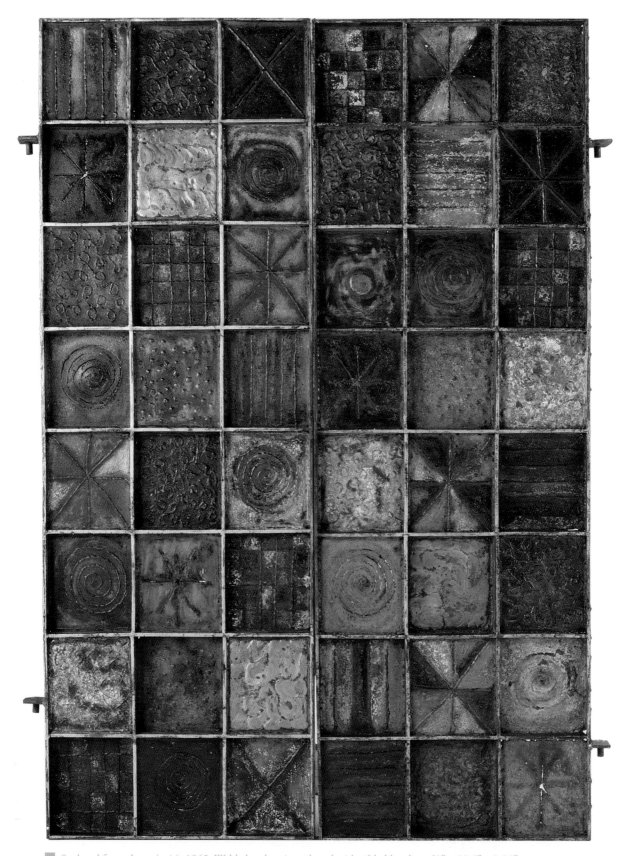

■ Sculpted front doors (pair), 1965. Welded and patinated steel with gilded borders. 60" x 20.5" x 2.25".
Courtesy of Rago Arts and Auction Center.

■ Sculpted panel, 1970. Welded and patinated steel. 24" x 4" x 24". *Courtesy of Wright.*

■ Sculpted panel, 1974. Welded and patinated steel with gilded details. 48.5" x 59.75". *Courtesy of Rago Arts and Auction Center.*

Sculpted panel room divider, 1967. Welded and patinated steel. Paint and gold leaf. 72.75" x 96" x 4". *Courtesy of Rago Arts and Auction Center.*

■ Detail. Sculpted panel room divider,1967. *Courtesy of Rago Arts and Auction Center.*

■ Detail. Sculpted panel room divider, 1967. *Courtesy of Rago Arts and Auction Center.*

■ Detail. Sculpted panel room divider, 1967. *Courtesy of Rago Arts and Auction Center.*

Sculpted front cabinet with two doors, 1972. Welded and patinated steel with gold leaf. 82" x 36" x 20". *Courtesy of Rago Arts and Auction Center.*

■ Detail. Sculpted front cabinet with two doors, 1972. *Courtesy of Rago Arts and Auction Center.*

■ Detail. Sculpted front cabinet with two doors, 1972. Interior with red paint, storage compartment and gold leaf drawers. *Courtesy of Rago Arts and Auction Center.*

■ Detail. Sculpted front cabinet with two doors, 1972. *Courtesy of Rago Arts and Auction Center.*

■ Sculpted front cabinet, c. 1960. Welded and patinated steel. Painted wood with gold leaf. Handles and gilt drawers by Phillip Lloyd Powell. 32.25" x 46.0125" x 24.25". *Courtesy of Sotheby's.*

■ Sculpted front, wall-mounted cabinet, 1968. Welded and patinated steel, gilded details with natural cleft slate top. 19.5" x 41" x 21". *Courtesy of Rago Arts and Auction Center.*

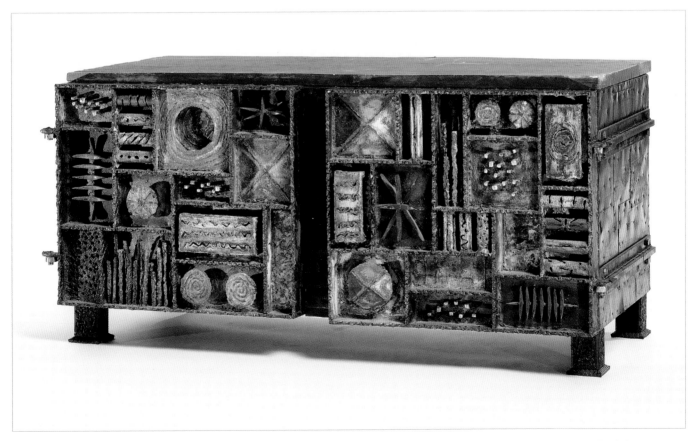

■ Sculpted front sideboard, 1969. Welded and patinated steel with gilt and natural cleft slate top. 25" x 53.5" x 22.5". *Courtesy of Sotheby's.*

■ Sculpted front cabinet [mounted on a steel base] with four doors, 1965. Red lacquer interior with felt lined shelves. Welded and patinated steel with enamel, bronze, brass, gold leaf, and lacquered wood. Natural cleft slate top. 99" x 24" x 22.5". Signed by both Evans and studio craftsman Cool (Robert Lee Thomas). *Courtesy of Todd Merrill 20th Century.*

Detail. Sculpted front wall-
mounted cabinet, 1973. *Courtesy
of Rago Arts and Auction Center.*

Sculpted front wall-mounted cabinet,
1973. Welded and patinated steel. With
natural cleft slate top. 21" x 72" x 18".
Courtesy of Rago Arts and Auction Center.

43

Sculpted front cabinet with two doors, 1966. Welded and patinated steel, copper patchwork with gold leaf. 89.5" x 30" x 22". *Courtesy of Rago Arts and Auction Center.*

Detail. Sculpted front cabinet with two doors, 1966. Gold leaf. *Courtesy of Rago Arts and Auction Center.*

Detail. Sculpted front cabinet with two doors, 1966. Paul Evans signature. *Courtesy of Rago Arts and Auction Center.*

Detail. Sculpted front cabinet with two doors, 1966. *Courtesy of Rago Arts and Auction Center.*

■ A monumental sculpted panel suspended by a metal frame, c. 1965. Approximately 85" x 41" x 22".
Courtesy of Dorsey Reading.

■ Sculpted front wall-mounted cabinet with two doors, 1969. Interior storage slots. Welded and patinated steel with gilt and enameled. Natural cleft slate top. 75" x 23.25 x 22.5". *Courtesy of Wright.*

■ Sculpted front, wall-mounted cabinet [set on a base] with four doors and interior shelves, 1966. Welded and patinated steel with enamel, bronze, brass, gold leaf, and lacquered wood. Natural cleft slate top. 99" x 24" x 36.5". *Courtesy of Wright.*

Sculpted front cabinet [mounted on a steel base] with four doors and felt lined interior shelves, 1968. Welded and patinated steel with enamel, bronze, brass, gold leaf, and lacquered wood. Natural cleft slate top. 100" x 24" x 31". *Courtesy of Todd Merrill 20th Century.*

Sculpted coffee table, c. 1960. Welded and patinated steel with enamel. Glass top. 54" x 20" x 15.25". *Courtesy of Wright.*

Detail. Sculpted coffee table, c. 1960. *Courtesy of Peter and Jennifer Gleeson, Seattle, Washington.*

■ Detail. Underside of sculpted coffee table, c. 1960. *Courtesy of Peter and Jennifer Gleeson, Seattle, Washington.*

■ Detail. Sculpted coffee table, c. 1960. *Courtesy of Peter and Jennifer Gleeson, Seattle, Washington.*

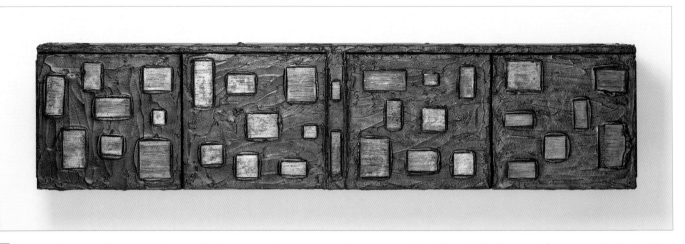

■ Sculpted bronze wall-mounted cabinet with four doors and an interior with three adjustable shelves, 1969. Natural cleft slate top. 96.5" x 20.5" x 22.5". *Courtesy of Wright.*

■ Sculpted credenza with four doors, c. 1972. Welded steel with enamel. Natural cleft slate top. 96" x 22" x 30". *Courtesy of Wright.*

■ Sculpted wall-mounted cabinet with two doors and two storage compartments with interior adjustable shelves, c. 1972. Welded steel with enamel. Natural cleft slate top. 48.5" x 16.5" x 17.5". *Courtesy of Wright.*

Wavy front wall-mounted cabinet, 1966. Welded and patinated steel with natural cleft slate top. 21" x 72" x 22.5". *Courtesy of Rago Arts and Auction Center.*

Detail. Wavy front wall-mounted cabinet, 1966. *Courtesy of Rago Arts and Auction Center.*

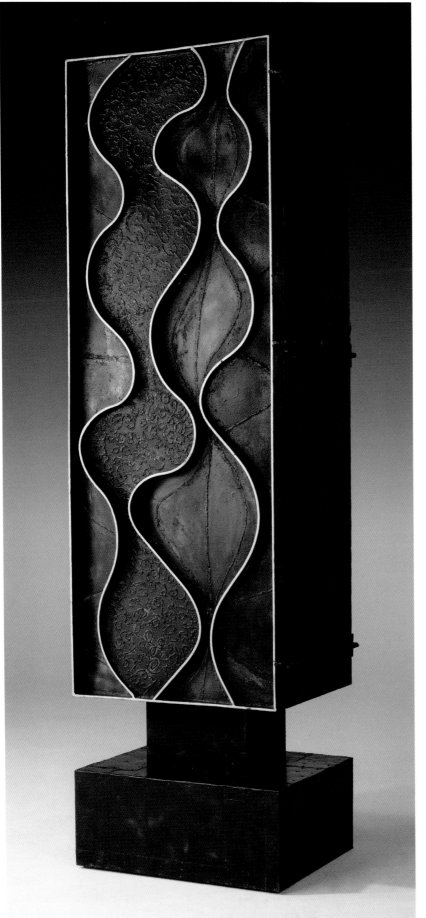

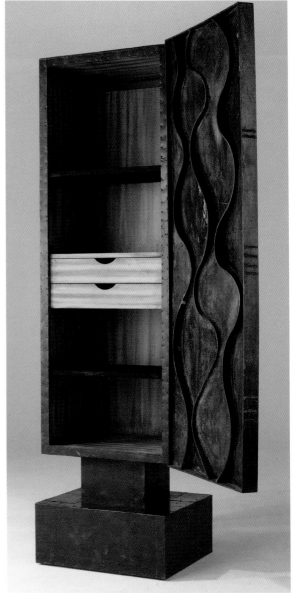

■ Detail. Wavy front cabinet. Interior with painted wood shelves and drawers, c. 1977–1978. *Courtesy of Rago Arts and Auction Center.*

■ Wavy front cabinet on pedestal base, c. 1977–1978. Welded and patinated steel with gilded door. 84" x 24" x 21.5". *Courtesy of Rago Arts and Auction Center.*

■ Sculpted bronze cabinet with two doors, c. 1969. Fabric covered base. 78.375" x 21.25" x 21.25". *Courtesy of Sotheby's.*

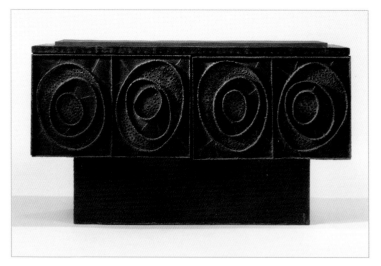

Sculpted cabinet on pedestal base, c. 1967. Two doors with two interior shelves. Welded steel with enamel and gilt. Natural cleft slate top. 48.25" x 19.5" x 27". *Courtesy of Wright.*

Hanging light fixture, 1964. Banded and perforated copper with verdigris patina. 22.25" x 11.5". *Courtesy of Rago Arts and Auction Center.*

Verdigris cooper loop wall-mounted cabinet, c. 1960 (with Carlo Scarpa glass vase and Harry Bertoia sonambient sculpture). Patinated cooper and bronze with gold leaf. 59.875" x 48.5" x 18.25". *Courtesy of Wright.*

■ Three-paneled room divider, c. 1957. Patinated steel with gold leaf edges. 90" x 26" x 8.5" (each panel). *Courtesy of Rago Arts and Auction Center.*

Barrel-shaped chair, 1973. Patinated steel with suede upholstery. 28.5" x 29" x 22.5". *Courtesy of Rago Arts and Auction Center.*

Ribbed ashtray, 1966. Experimental form. Cast aluminum. 2.5" x 9". *Courtesy of Rago Arts and Auction Center.*

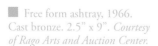
Free form ashtray, 1966. Cast bronze. 2.5" x 9". *Courtesy of Rago Arts and Auction Center.*

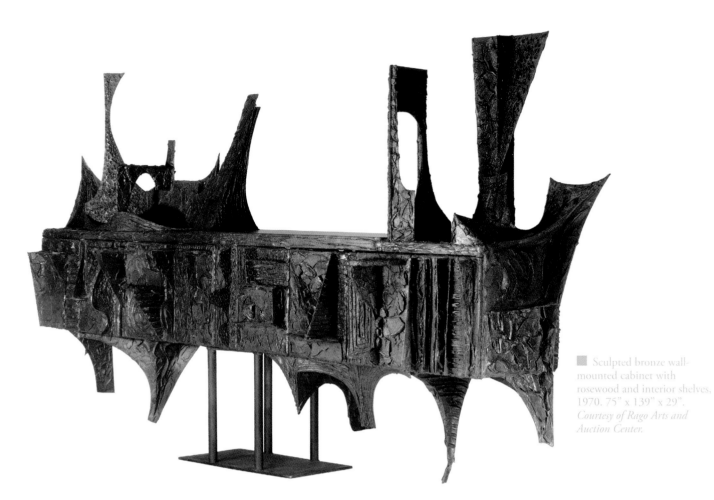

Sculpted bronze wall-mounted cabinet with rosewood and interior shelves, 1970. 75" x 139" x 29". *Courtesy of Rago Arts and Auction Center.*

Detail. Sculpted bronze wall-mounted cabinet, 1970. *Courtesy of Rago Arts and Auction Center.*

■ Sculpted bronze armchair, 1967. Original cowhide upholstery with two circular cushions. 52.5" x 31.5" x 29".
Courtesy of Christie's.

Sculpted bronze cabinet, 1970. Two doors with two sliding shelves. 36" x 26" x 75". *Courtesy of Wright.*

Sculpted bronze wall unit with glass, 1969/1971. Prototype chair with upholstery. 96" x 14.5" x 81". *Courtesy of Wright.*

■ Sculpted bronze sofa with upholstery, c. 1970. 72" x 22" x 30". *Courtesy of Wright.*

■ Sculpted bronze furniture group, c. 1970. *Courtesy of Dorsey Reading.*

Sculptures

In the early 1960s, when Evans was producing the *Sculpted Steel Series* and smaller utility pieces, he started making sculptures. The medium gave Evans the opportunity to experiment with shape, scale, and surface, and to apply his creativity to the design of purely decorative 3-D objects. He was more hands-on, literally and figuratively, with the sculptures than with any other work.

He completed 30 to 35 sculptures, the majority of them made between 1962 and 1968. They generally predate his involvement with Directional. Most of the sculptures were sold in Evans's New Hope Showroom. Although the earliest sculptures were commissions Evans and Powell worked on together, which were usually made with walnut and metal, Evans continued to make a small number of sculptures through the early 1970s.

■ Paul Evans, c. 1965. *Courtesy of Dorsey Reading.*

■ Wall-hanging sculpture. Welded and patinated steel, copper with gold-leaf details. 42.5" x 71" x 7". *Courtesy of Rago Arts and Auction Center.*

Fountain sculpture, c. 1956. Welded and wrought steel. 43.25" x 43" x 11.5". *Courtesy of Rago Arts and Auction Center.*

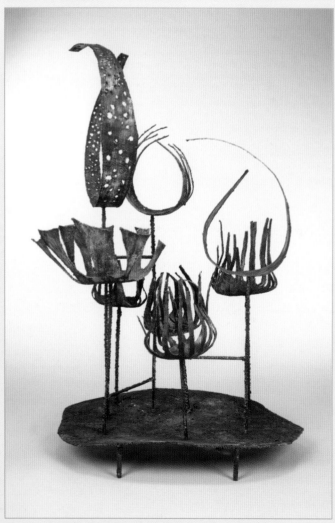

Cut, welded, and patinated steel and copper sculpture, c. 1965. 33.5" x 23.5" x 51". *Courtesy of Wright.*

Candelabrum, c. 1955. Steel and patinated copper. 26" x 17" x 37.5". *Courtesy of Wright.*

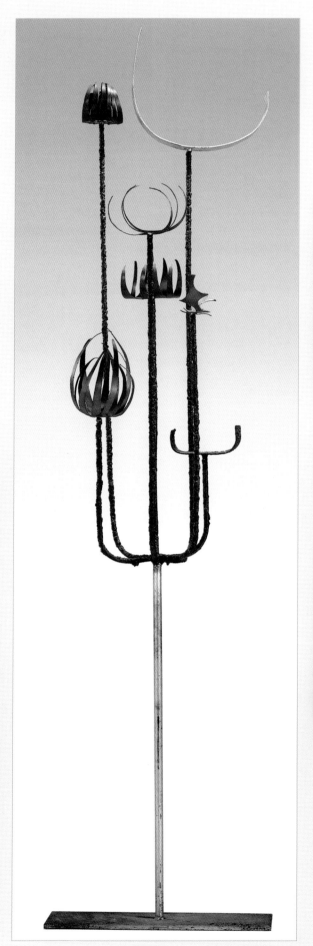

A welded and patinated steel and copper sculpture on a gilded stand, 1968. 68.5" x 17.5" x 38". *Courtesy of Rago Arts and Auction Center.*

Detail. Cut, welded and patinated steel sculpture, c. 1965. *Courtesy of Wright.*

Directional

Paul Evans began designing for Directional Furniture in 1964. B. G. Mesberg the founder of Directional was looking for a new designer to replace Paul McCobb, who had a falling out with the company. Although there were other designers working for Directional at the time, McCobb's departure left a gap creatively and financially. Prior to Evans joining Directional, California designers Kip Stewart and Stewart MacDonald created a line of beds and tables for the company. Another California designer, Milo Baughman, best known today his op-art tabletop design, created his "Country Villa" line for Directional. Baughman was largely responsible for Directional's upholstered pieces. Later, when Baughman's relationship with the company ended in the late 1960s, Evans developed a line of upholstered furniture for Directional.

Mesberg had seen Evans's work at America House, and knew Evans had a studio. They met and agreed Evans would design a series of tables. Mesberg felt it was a step up for Directional to offer handcrafted, studio-designed pieces. The two men developed a good relationship and got along very well. At the time, Evans and Mesberg had no idea the line would grow to 800 different pieces produced between 1964 and 1982.

The first line Evans did for Directional was a group of 5 or 6 small copper and steel coffee tables with glass tops. The tables were scheduled for introduction at the spring 1964 "Market Week" industry trade show in Highpoint, North Carolina. Evans drove all night to Highpoint in the family station wagon. When he arrived, Directional decided not to put the tables on the showroom floor. This upset Evans and made him more determined to show the tables, so he drove to New York to meet with Mesberg. That resulted in having the tables shipped from Highpoint and placed in the Directional showroom in New York City. As soon as the tables arrived in the showroom, they began selling and were an immediate success. In the first month, orders were placed for 30-35 coffee tables. Evans only made the metal bases. Directional provided the glass tops.

The success of the tables led to Directional requesting more pieces and different designs. Thus, the "Patchwork" line was introduced with copper and pewter. The first piece was a shelf with a slate top and mirror. The line expanded to tables, cabinets, and smaller items such as boxes covered in copper.

Executive desk with return, c. 1960. Five drawers, telephone mount, file slots, and storage compartments. Steel panels cut and welded. Patinated. With lacquered wood, enamel, and gilt. Natural cleft slate top. 108" x 60" x 37". 21" x 72" x 22.5". *Courtesy of Wright.*

■ Patchwork occasional table, c. 1970. Bronze, copper, and pewter with natural cleft slate top. 18.25" x 13.125" x 13.125".
Courtesy of Sotheby's.

 Patchwork cube chair, c. 1970. Copper and painted steel base with upholstery. 28" x 30" x 30". *Courtesy of Rago Arts and Auction Center.*

Directional catalog page, c. 1969. Patchwork parson-type cocktail and side table. Steel, bronze, copper, and pewter with natural cleft slate top. *Courtesy of Objects USA.*

■ Patchwork chairs with castors, c. 1970. Bronze, copper, pewter, and steel. Approximate height 33". *Courtesy of Sotheby's.*

Patchwork cube chairs with blue leather upholstery, c. 1968. This is the only set of verdigris copper cube Evans designed. 30.5" x 32.25" x 34.5. *Courtesy of Wright.*

Patchwork cube chair, c. 1970.
Copper and painted steel base
with upholstery. 28" x 30" x 30".
Courtesy of Dorsey Reading.

Patchwork cube cabinet with two doors, c. 1970.
Interior has open storage compartment. Welded and
patinated steel. 31" x 31" x 26.5". *Courtesy of Wright.*

■ Cube occasional tables, 1967. Welded and enameled steel with natural cleft slate top. 14.5" x 14.5" x 18.5". *Courtesy of Wright.*

■ Patchwork console with mirror, c. 1971. Bronze, copper, steel and glass with natural cleft slate top. 60" x 13" x 35.5". *Courtesy of Wright.*

■ Console with mirror, 1971. Welded and enameled steel, copper with natural cleft slate top. 60" x 13" x 6". *Courtesy of Wright.*

■ Patchwork ice bucket, c. 1970. Bronze, copper, and steel. 10.25" x 10.25" x 6.25". *Courtesy of Wright.*

Lamp table, c. 1965. Welded and enameled steel with glass. 32" x 29". *Courtesy of Wright.*

Patchwork adjustable stool, 1965. Welded and patinated steel. 23" x 23" x 32.5". *Courtesy of Wright.*

Adjustable stool, c. 1965. Welded and enameled steel with upholstery. 19" x 19". *Courtesy of Wright.*

Lighting fixture, c. 1970. Welded, patinated steel and bronze. 30" x 30" x 32.5". *Courtesy of Wright.*

Directional catalog page, 1965. *Courtesy of Dorsey Reading.*

Cabinet with two doors, 1967. Welded and enameled steel with natural cleft slate top. 48" x 20.75" x 32.5". *Courtesy of Wright.*

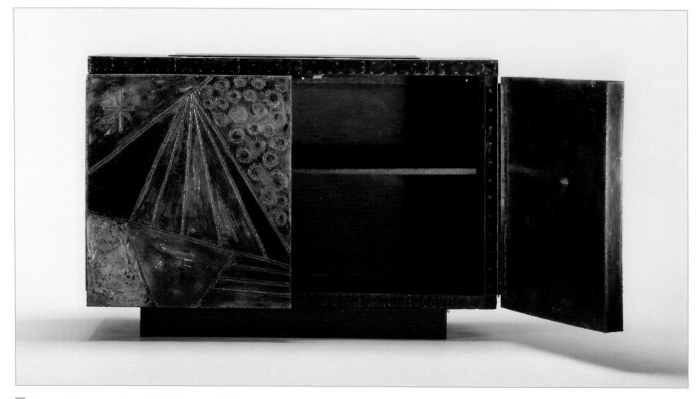

Detail. Cabinet interior, 1967. *Courtesy of Wright.*

■ Cabinet with four doors, 1973. Welded and enameled steel with natural cleft slate top. 96.5" x 22" x 31.5". *Courtesy of Wright.*

■ Cabinet with two bi-fold doors, 1973. Welded and enameled steel with natural cleft slate top. Interior adjustable shelf. 72" x 21.5" x 31". *Courtesy of Wright.*

Stools, c. 1971. Welded and enameled steel with upholstery. 17" x 17" x 18. *Courtesy of Wright.*

Coffee table, 1972. Welded, patinated steel, and bronze with glass. 48.25" x 16". *Courtesy of Wright.*

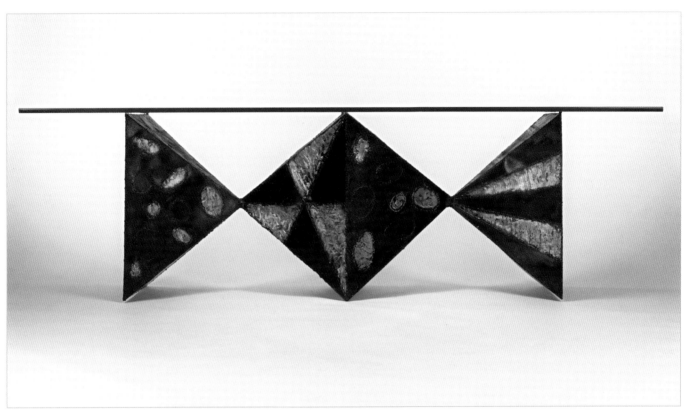

■ Dining table, c. 1965. Brass, bronze, and glass. 95.5" x 48.25" x 29.75". *Courtesy of Wright.*

■ Wall-mounted cabinet with two doors and interior adjustable shelf, c. 1965.
48.5" x 17" x 17.5". *Courtesy of Wright.*

Patchwork Sculptures

Each one of Evans's sculptures was unique. On only two or three occasions was a variation created. Working from sketches, Evans frequently used a ball shape in his sculptures: round, squat, or pointed. The ball sculptures ranged in size from twelve inches to six feet. The sculptures were hollow with an interior structure consisting of bent 3/8" square steel rods. This armature defined the shape of the sculpture, and the metal surface was then braised or welded to the form. Most of the sculptures were done with a patchwork metal finish. Some sculptures had white paint with an acid finish, others were braised, and some were made of brass or bronze. Most were verdigris copper and treated with acid to start the verdigris process, which created a patina. Sometimes the surface was etched with lines or a pattern. The sculptures were seldom signed, especially the verdigris copper pieces.

◼ Detail. Free form sculpture, c. 1965. *Courtesy of Wright.*

◼ Free form sculpture, c. 1965. Welded and patinated steel. 33.5" x 31" x 6". *Courtesy of Wright.*

■ Pie sculpture, 1971. Etched
verdigris copper. 13" x 16" x 4.5".
Courtesy of Wright.

■ Wing sculpture, c. 1968. One
of two. Verdigris copper patchwork
over steel armature. 28" x 10" x 29".
Courtesy of Wright.

■ Planter, 1968. Welded steel patchwork. 19" x 16". *Courtesy of Rago Arts and Auction Center.*

■ Ball sculpture, c. 1965. Verdigris copper patchwork over steel armature. 16" x 19.5". *Courtesy of Wright.*

■ "Onion" sculpture, 1965. Considered the largest sculpture Evans produced. Steel patchwork over steel armature. Created for his friend and studio partner, Phillip Powell. 76" x 67" on 8" x 30" x 20" base. *Courtesy of Rago Arts and Auction Center.*

■ Three-piece diamond-form sculpture, 1973. Verdigris copper. 30" x 12" x 8". *Courtesy of Wright.*

It was common for Evans to work on 3 or 4 sculptures at a time, although finishing took considerably longer and some were never completed.

Evans's sculptures were typically done as an expression, a departure from the other activities of his studio, often without a deliberate marketing purpose. Over the course of his career Evans received several commissions for sculptures and always enjoyed the medium, as he personally worked the shapes and surface texture.

■ Sculpture, 1964. Steel and brass. Dimensions unknown. *Courtesy of Dorsey Reading.*

■ Sculpture. Steel and brass, 1965. Dimensions unknown. *Courtesy of Dorsey Reading.*

■ Sculpture, 1966. Steel and brass. Approximate height 72". *Courtesy of Dorsey Reading.*

■ Sculpture, 1966. Steel and brass. Approximate height 72".
Courtesy of Dorsey Reading.

and exploded views showing assembly and sub-assembly. The specs were done in-house, based on built, finished pieces. During production the pieces would move through the various departments in the factory, depending on whether it was wood or metal, based on the specs.

In addition to showrooms for the trade, Evans's Directional pieces were available in the mid-1970s through retailers in New York such as Altman's, Bloomingdale's, and W. & J. Sloane. Evans's Directional pieces at the company's West Coast "Boutique," which opened in 1968 on Beverly Boulevard in Los Angeles, featured Evans's custom made bronze doors. The showroom did not achieve the same level of success as other locations, although there were sales of steel and bronze pieces. This was attributed to the difficulty of competing with established designers and decorators in the market.

Part of the appeal of Evans's Directional pieces was the ability to choose different options, allowing buyers to customize their order. If a customer wanted drawers inside a cabinet or if they wanted a configuration to accommodate a stereo, the factory could make the changes. There were fees for the various alterations customers requested, yet it was very common to make modifications.

Directional liked Evans's work signed, so many pieces were signed "PE." Others were initialed by the craftsmen who worked on the piece in addition to the "PE." Evans did not mind the second set of initials and believed it gave everyone a sense of pride. Dorsey Reading signed most of the pieces. Evans did not care if his name was on the finished product or not. A date was often signed, too, such as "74" for 1974. All pieces typically had a brass or chrome plate label, such as: "Paul Evans," "Paul Evans for Directional" or "An Original Paul Evans."

At the height of production for Directional in 1975 and 1976, Evans employed 88 people. The factory ran two shifts, while a separate group worked on only custom, studio pieces.

During Evans's time with Directional, the company continued to offer furniture by other designers, but the popularity of Evans designs was dominant and singularly responsible for Directional's profits.

After Mesberg died in 1977, his son ran Directional. This caused many changes, leading to the end of Evans's relationship with the company. The market was also changing and Directional was becoming less competitive. Its product lines in the last years were not successful, and the company was losing stature. In 1981 Evans decided to open his own showroom in New York City. He made his last pieces for Directional in 1982.

In the early years, the pieces for Directional were made in Evans's Lambertville, New Jersey, workshop. Then, in 1970, Evans set up a factory in Plumsteadville, Pennsylvania, about 10 miles away from Lambertville to do production for Directional. Prototyping and ongoing development of custom made-to-order studio pieces, which began in 1959, remained in Lambertville.

The factory in Plumsteadville, previously a golf ball factory, was 30,000 square feet and accounted for 80 to 85 percent of Evans's business. Everything was done in-house and nothing was subcontracted. This assured Evans 100 percent control, which prevented people from finding out about techniques and how pieces were made.

For each line, a set of design specs, with detailed manufacturing drawings, showed the steps and sequence to make each piece. This included a cut list of materials such as wood, metal, etc.,

The Directional Lines

Each product line for Directional was assigned a series number. The progression of numbers indicates the growth and variety of Evans's designs, and the ongoing requests from Directional to create new pieces. Since several product lines were made simultaneously, a cross section was available. Over time certain pieces within a line were phased out or replaced with a new design. As always Directional offered "custom-designed variations, either in size, or in combinations of materials." Many elaborate Directional custom-ordered pieces were ultimately Studio pieces and were Directional in name only.

11-99 (no 0-10)

These are Evans's earliest pieces for Directional, and include his first metal coffee and dining tables using copper, bronze and steel, copper, bronze, or pewter. The method of applying surface treatments on plywood or flake board frames began at this time for works that were not solid metal.

Cabinet interiors, including drawers and shelves were covered in a standard black formica regardless of the line.

Bronze 100

The 1968 catalog for the Bronze line was the first one to show only Evans's work, separate from Directional's other designers. For many of the early catalogs, a room was set up in Evans's studio to photograph the designs, shot mostly by local photographer Peter Page.

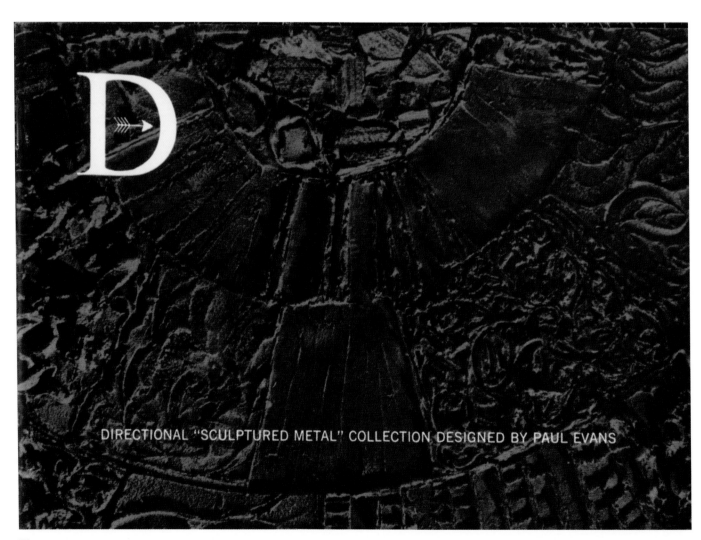

DIRECTIONAL "SCULPTURED METAL" COLLECTION DESIGNED BY PAUL EVANS

Directional catalog with detail of wall-mounted disk bar, c. 1969. *Courtesy of Dorsey Reading.*

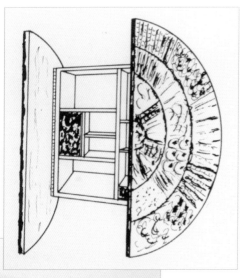

■ Directional catalog rendering
of wall-mounted disk bar, c. 1969.
Courtesy of Dorsey Reading.

■ Sculpted bronze wall-mounted disk bar with interior cabinets, c. 1969. 15" x 72" (diameter). *Courtesy of Wright.*

Directional catalog page, c. 1969. Wall unit with bronze pilasters and bronze tinted glass. *Courtesy of Objects USA.*

Directional catalog page, c. 1969. Sculpted bronze wall-mounted cabinet with four doors. Natural cleft slate top. [Framed Joan Miro print above] *Courtesy of Objects USA.*

■ Sculpted bronze chair with orange crushed velvet upholstery, 1965. 31.75" x 28.75" x 24.75". *Courtesy of Wright.*

Sculpted bronze cabinets with two natural cleft slate tops, c. 1970. Each has two doors and an interior adjustable shelf. 48.5" x 21.25" x 31.25". *Courtesy of Wright.*

Directional catalog page, 1965. *Courtesy of Dorsey Reading.*

■ Directional catalog page, 1965.
Courtesy of Dorsey Reading.

■ Directional catalog page, 1965.
Courtesy of Dorsey Reading.

■ Sculpted bronze occasional tables with rosewood top, c. 1965. Described in the Directional catalog as "Tree trunk tables." 15" x 18.5" and 20" x 12". *Courtesy of Rago Arts and Auction Center.*

■ Directional catalog page, 1965. *Courtesy of Dorsey Reading.*

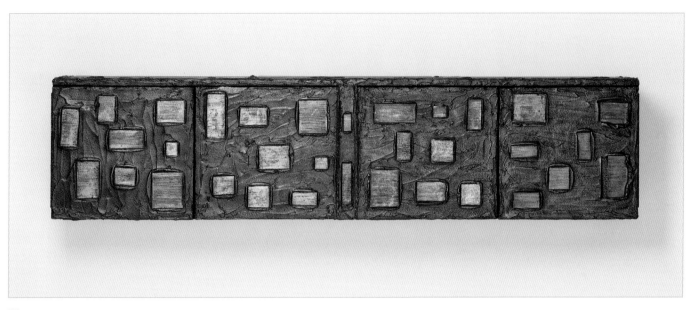

■ Sculpted bronze wall-mounted cabinet with four doors, 1969. Natural cleft slate top. The interior has three adjustable shelves. 96.5" x 20.5" x 22.5". *Courtesy of Wright.*

■ Directional catalog page, c. 1969. Bronze dining group with "stalagmite" table, upholstered chairs, and sculpted bronze, wall-mounted cabinet with natural cleft slate top. *Courtesy of Objects USA.*

Flat sculpted bronze armchair (unproduced
furniture line), 1969. With upholstery. 37" x 26" x 31".
Courtesy of Wright.

Argente armoire with two doors and an interior shelf, c. 1969. Welded and enameled aluminum. 36.5" x 21.5" x 80". *Courtesy of Wright.*

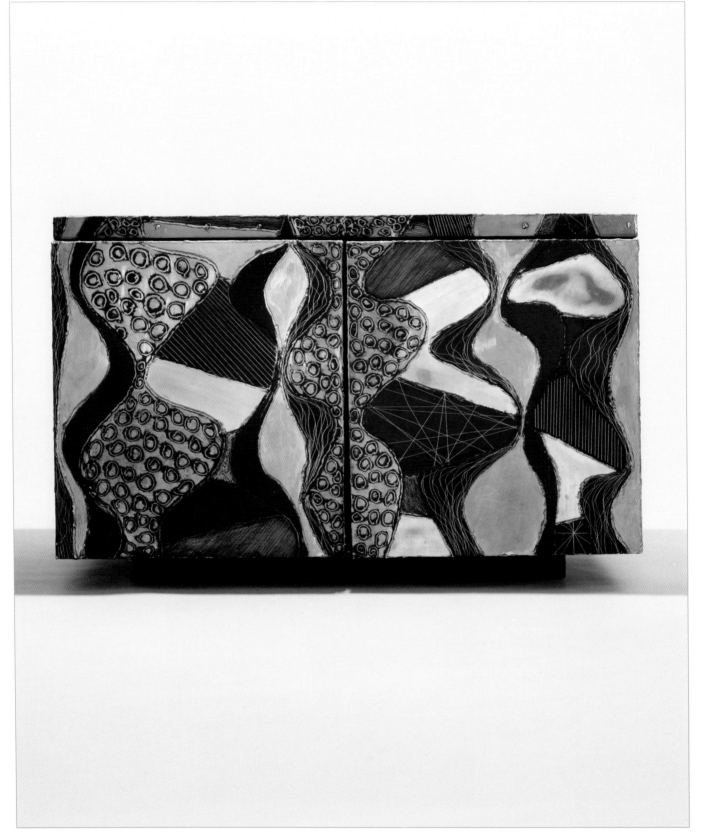

Argente cabinet with two doors and an interior storage compartment, 1972. Welded and enameled aluminum, with natural cleft slate top. 50" x 22" x 31". *Courtesy of Wright.*

Argente cabinet with two doors and an adjustable interior shelf, 1969. An example of how the same piece in a furniture line was often designed and treated differently. Welded and enameled aluminum. 48" x 19.5" x 32". *Courtesy of Wright.*

Argente sideboard with two doors and eight interior drawers. 1968. Welded and enameled aluminum with natural cleft slate top. 32" x 84" x 21". *Courtesy of Converso.*

■ Detail. Argente sideboard with two doors and eight interior drawers, 1968. *Courtesy of Converso.*

Detail. Argente sideboard with two doors and eight interior drawers, 1968. *Courtesy of Converso.*

Argente box, c. 1972. Welded and enameled aluminum. 6.25" x 16" x 8". *Courtesy of Rago Arts and Auction Center.*

Goup

Goup was an epoxy mainly applied to bronze pieces, and some aluminum, with a rag, or smeared on with the sharp edge of a trowel. Different experiments were tried before the goup technique was finalized. The first attempts to create a textured shape and surface were done with a zinc spray, which turned a silver color. This color coating only lasted four or five months so it was not used.

Glass beads and plaster was another experiment to create surface texture. Beads were broken, which turned out to be costly. However, it achieved the desired granular effect and lasted longer than other techniques, but when the plaster was painted with a gold spray it did not look natural, it too was dropped.

The final experiments with epoxy, hardener, and sand, led to the continued use of the goup technique. The recipe for the compound was not precise. Sometimes it was made stiffer or thicker by adding more sand. Sand gave it texture and made it easy to shape and apply. Once it was applied to the surface of a piece, it was sandblasted to eliminate the sheen. If it was not sandblasted properly, the piece was redone. Each person working with goup had his or her own way of applying the material. Since no set pattern was imposed, personal variations ensured a unique, hand done quality.

Large sections of goup, from the previous day were hit with a hammer to make smaller bits. These smaller parts were pushed into the epoxy compound and became part of the piece.

Argente

Evans on-going, extensive trial and error experimentation led to the Argente line that was based on a technique for using 1/8" thick aluminum sheets. The aluminum was shaped, blackened with ink so it was solid black, sanded, buffed, and textured with a torch so the surface had a ripple effect. The fumes from welding the aluminum made it difficult to produce; even though air fans were used, those doing the welding kept cough drops in their mouths to stop the constant nose and throat irritation.

This technique-intensive line was offered with a slate top option and included cabinets, an armoire and a cube, which was typically used as a table. Evans also made a small group of sculptures with the Argente technique.

Argente Sculptures

Evans also created aluminum sculptures in the mid-1960s, using Argente, the black etch technique, based on the line of furniture he designed for Directional. Although only a few Argente sculptures were made, they were elaborate and technically more involved. The aluminum was shaped, then blackened with ink so it was solid black, sanded, buffed, and textured with a torch so the surface had a ripple effect.

One example of Argente is a *Pinwheel* sculpture, made in three circular, progressive pieces of different sizes and weights cut from a single sheet of aluminum. The three pieces were fitted and then individually welded. For this sculpture the 3/8" steel rod was forged and hammered on an anvil. The *Blooming Onion* sculpture employed a similar structure. Made for his friend Phillip Lloyd Powell, it is considered Evans's largest sculpture.

Argente sculpture from the *Sculptures in the Fields* series (Bucks County, Pennsylvania), c. 1965. Welded and enameled aluminum. 14" x 14" x 78". *Courtesy of Dorsey Reading.*

■ Argente *Pinwheel* sculpture from *Sculptures in the Field* series (Bucks County, Pennsylvania), c. 1968. Welded and enameled aluminum. 43.5" x 39.5" d x 73". *Courtesy of Wright.*

■ Detail. Argente *Pinwheel* sculpture from *Sculptures in the Field* series, c. 1968. *Courtesy of Wright.*

■ Argente sculpture from the *Sculptures in the Fields* series (Bucks County, Pennsylvania), c. 1965. Welded and enameled aluminum. Dimensions unknown. *Courtesy of Dorsey Reading.*

■ Argente sculpture from the *Sculptures in the Fields* series (Bucks County, Pennsylvania), c. 1965. Welded and enameled aluminum. Dimensions unknown. *Courtesy of Dorsey Reading.*

■ Detail. Argente sculpture from the *Sculptures in the Fields* series (Bucks County, Pennsylvania), c. 1965. Welded and enameled aluminum. Dimensions unknown. *Courtesy of Dorsey Reading.*

Chrome 200

The Chrome line, also known as "Cityscape," was a set of five different pieces in steel, brass, nickel, or polished or brushed chrome. The line also included a bed, mirrors, tables, and various accessories.

Development of the line required many experiments to find the best solution for getting metal to stick to the surface of the wood framed pieces. Evans first tried heat sensitive adhesives, but the adhesives peeled. Eventually a tape with a tissue type layer became the lasting solution. The earliest chrome pieces, made before the tape technique, have a black rubber backing between the chrome and the wood.

Once all the components were in place, each chrome piece was ironed. A protective tissue prevented direct contact between the iron and chrome. The heat from the iron activated the contact cement between the backside of the metal and the wood surface underneath. After ironing, the protective tissue was removed and the piece was polished. In general, the polished metal pieces were easily damaged if mishandled or not cared for during use.

With Directional's need to continually offer new pieces, Evans created striking variations that resulted in an entirely new line. For marketing purposes Directional capitalized on the success of Cityscape and its name, and chose to call the new line Cityscape II. Between Cityscape I and II approximately 150 pieces were produced. Some all metal, some all wood and others a combination. Cityscape production ran from 1971 to 1981.

Cityscape II included faceted pieces (300 series) and burl and metal (400 series). Evans and those working with him in the studio made little reference to "Cityscape II." Instead they used the more descriptive names (another situation occurred with "sculptured" used in Directional marketing, though "sculpted" was used in the studio).

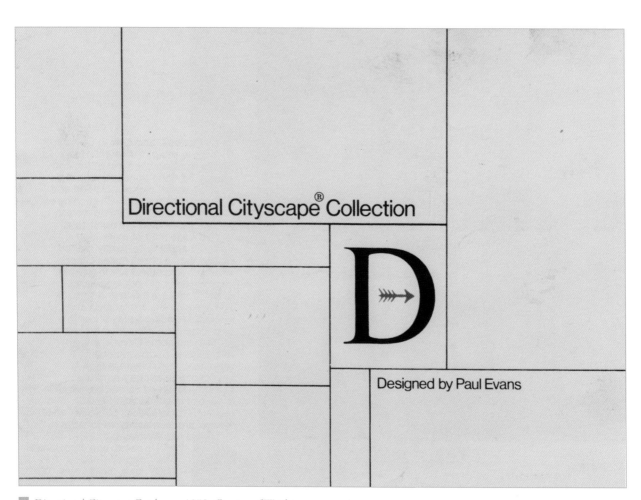

Directional Cityscape Catalog, c. 1975. *Courtesy of Wright.*

Prototype for Cityscape furniture line, c. 1975. Fewer than ten of this particular suite were produced (and nine in brass). Numerous accessories and variations evolved from the line. Chrome plated steel on wood. 105" x 24.75 x 62.75"
Courtesy of Wright.

Cityscape chests, each with two doors and interior drawers, c. 1975. Chrome plated steel on wood. 34.25" x 20.5" x 26.25".
Courtesy of Wright.

■ Cityscape cantilevered, L-shaped table, c. 1975. Satin-bronze and chrome plated steel on wood. 15.25" x 60" x 48". *Courtesy of Todd Merrill 20th Century.*

■ Cityscape armchairs with leather upholstery, c. 1975. Chrome plated steel on wood. 24" x 31" x 30". *Courtesy of Wright.*

Directional catalog page, c. 1975. *Courtesy of Dorsey Reading.*

Cityscape dining chairs, 1975. Brass with upholstery. 24" x 27" x 34". *Courtesy of Wright.*

■ Cityscape table base, c. 1975. With brass. Chrome plated steel on wood. 34.5" x 23" x 27.5". *Courtesy of Wright.*

■ Cityscape bookshelf with brass and glass shelves, c. 1975. Chrome plated steel on wood. 37" x 10" x 90.5". *Courtesy of Wright.*

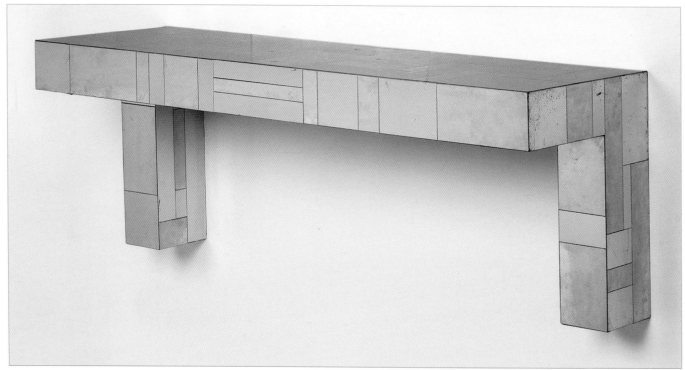

■ Cityscape wall-mounted shelf, c. 1975. With brass. Chrome plated steel on wood. 48" x 16" x 18.25". *Courtesy of Wright.*

Cityscape headboard with six electrical outlets along interior, c. 1975. Chrome plated steel on wood. 82" x 19" x 52.25". *Courtesy of Wright.*

Cityscape canopy, four-poster bed, 1975. For either a full, queen or king size bed. *Courtesy of Wright.*

Cityscape love sofas, c. 1975. Chrome plated steel on wood. Offered in various sizes. Tufted upholstery. 64.5" x 36.5" x 28". *Courtesy of Wright.*

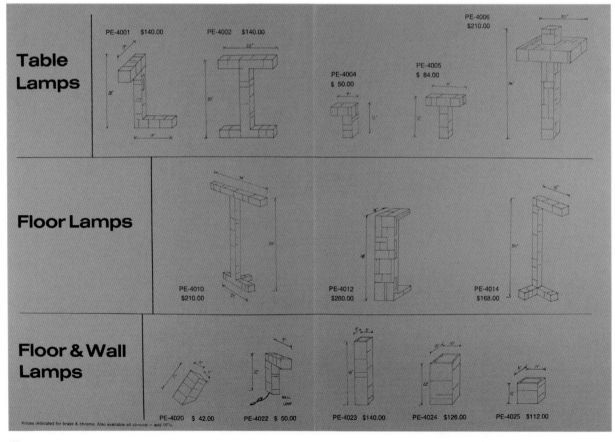

Cityscape lamp options, c. 1975. *Courtesy of Wright.*

■ Cityscape table lamps, c. 1975. With brass. Chrome plated steel on wood. 7" x 36". *Courtesy of Wright.*

■ Cityscape candle holder, assorted boxes, and cubes, c. 1975. Chrome plated steel on wood with brass. *Courtesy of Wright.*

Faceted 300

For the Faceted pieces, fiberglass molds were filled with high-density foam, a strong, light weight material which Evans literally used as building blocks. These were sealed with bolts. The foam was covered with wood or metal and attached to cabinets and other pieces.

In the early stages of development, the high-density foam caused the molds to blow up and become unusable. After further experiments, the correct amount of hardener was added to the foam mixture, which prevented it from expanding too much.

There were nine different sizes and form shapes for the faceted pieces. By turning and changing the orientation of each piece, a highly varied look was created. It was a time-consuming process to ensure all the pieces were flush with each other to avoid gaps. All the sections were pre-fitted before they were attached. This meant each piece, if it was covered with chrome, had to be fitted together before the first part was attached. Each piece was then removed and marked, and had the chrome applied individually. Some of table legs and hinges were also made with the high-density foam.

Larger faceted pieces could have over forty-five angled surfaces. Directional promoted this aspect of the design in catalogs stating it offered "a play of depth and dimension"

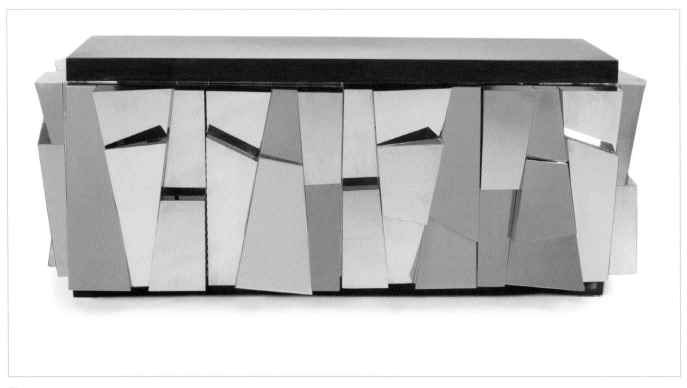

■ Faceted cabinet with two doors and interior storage compartment with adjustable shelf, c. 1970. Chrome plated steel, lacquered wood. 84" x 24" x 32". *Courtesy of Wright.*

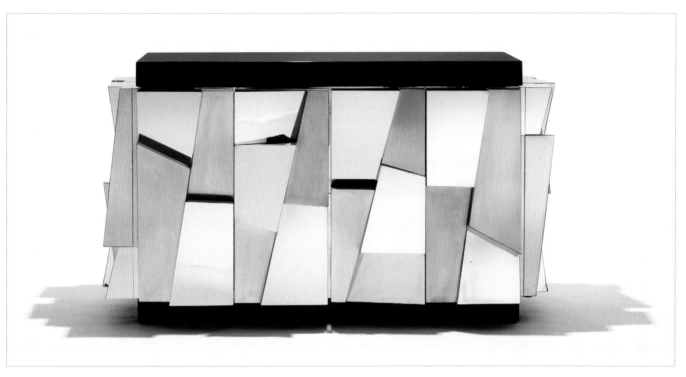

■ Faceted cabinet with two doors, c. 1970. Chrome plated steel. 58" x 25" x 32". *Courtesy of Wright.*

■ Faceted cabinet with two bi-fold doors, interior storage compartments, and adjustable shelf, c. 1970. Brass with maple burl. 82" x 24" x 32". *Courtesy of Wright.*

■ Faceted dining table, c. 1970. Chrome plated steel, walnut burl, and glass. 84" x 48" x 28.75". *Courtesy of Wright.*

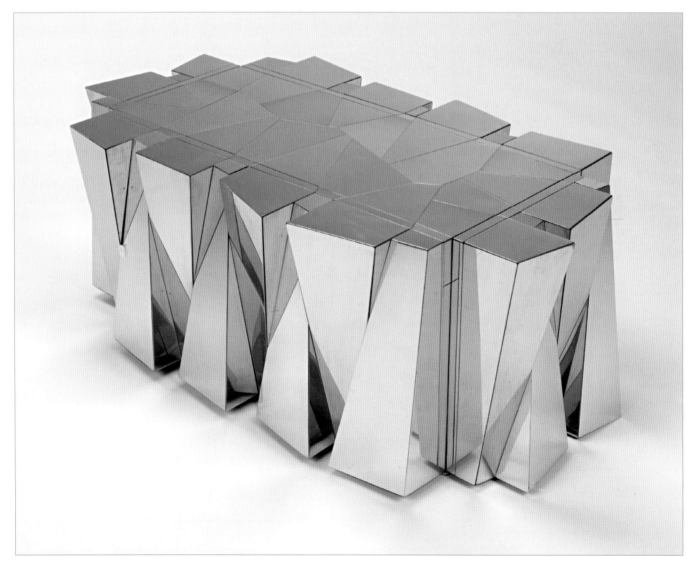

■ Faceted coffee table, c. 1970. Chrome plated steel with brass. 23" x 41" x 15.25". *Courtesy of Wright.*

Burl and Metal 400

The walnut burl pieces were selected directly from logs, after which they were treated and cut into a walnut veneer. Sanding and sheering with a custom-made double-bladed tool kept the edges straight and undamaged. After the pieces were cut, they were held together with masking tape then fitted to the surface, such as a table or cabinet. After fitting they were removed and contact cement was applied to both the back of the taped burl sections and the surface of the piece. The burls were then returned to the surface. The direct contact between the back of the veneer and the surface made a lasting bond that did not require heat.

Once the burl was set, the masking tape on the top side was removed and the piece was sanded to remove any imperfections. The piece was then sprayed with a sealer. When it dried, several layers of satin lacquer were applied. This would sit overnight and the next day the metal hardware was attached before shipping.

Other burls included olive ash and English oak. Customers had several color choices if they wanted the burl painted instead of keeping a natural finish.

There were times when the Evans factory had problems with the finish and would consult with Martin Guitar Co. Martin was using the identical lacquers as Evans and both companies shared information about getting rid of contamination or undesired ripple effects. It was usually obvious if the finish was not right, although the cause was not readily known, and could change from day to day.

The burl pieces involved the most technique and time to produce because there were so many more steps than the other lines.

Detail. Burl and polished chrome credenza, c. 1973. *Courtesy of Wright.*

Burl and polished chrome credenza with six doors, four interior drawers, and four adjustable shelves. c. 1973. Chrome plated steel with Olive Ash burl and wood. 94.5" x 21.25" x 32". *Courtesy of Wright.*

Directional catalog page, c. 1975. *Courtesy of Dorsey Reading.*

Burl and polished chrome wall-mounted cabinet with four doors and two interior adjustable shelves, c. 1973 (with Harry Bertoia *Bush* sculpture). Chrome plated steel with maple burl. 57" x 21" x 23". *Courtesy of Wright.*

Burl and polished chrome dining table, c. 1973. Chrome plated steel with elm burl. 72.5" x 40" x 30". *Courtesy of Wright.*

■ Burl and polished chrome dining table, c. 1973. Chrome plated steel with olive burl and glass. 95.5" x 46" x 29.5". *Courtesy of Wright.*

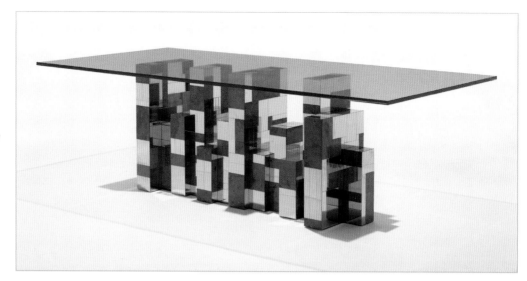

■ Burl and polished chrome credenza, with four doors and two interior adjustable shelves, c. 1973. Chrome plated steel with walnut burl. 76.5" x 21.25" x 32". *Courtesy of Wright.*

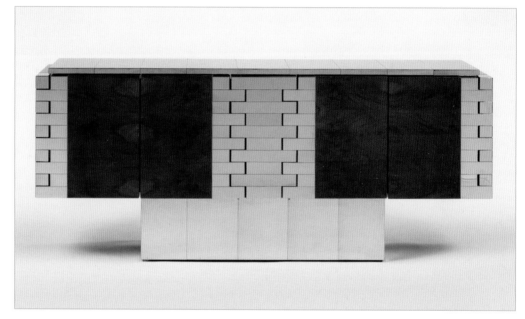

■ Burl and polished chrome credenza with four doors and two interior adjustable shelves, c. 1973. Chrome plated steel with elm burl. 84.25" x 20" x 32". *Courtesy of Wright.*

■ Directional catalog page, c. 1975. *Courtesy of Dorsey Reading.*

■ Burl and brass settee, c. 1970. Walnut with upholstery. 60" x 33" x 27". *Courtesy of Wright.*

Curved 500

Evolving from the straight, hard edges of the 400 Series, the 500 Series (produced from approximately 1970 to 1975) offered curvilinear styling using the same metals and techniques as the 400 Series. Some designs had leather accents. Molds for the line were made with fiberglass and steel, bolted together and injected with high-density foam.

■ Curved credenza with four doors with interior adjustable shelves, c. 1970. Burled wood. 31.75" x 83.75" x 20.5". *Courtesy of Rago Arts and Auction Center.*

■ Curved barrel desk and credenza, c. 1975. Walnut burl. *Courtesy of Dorsey Reading.*

■ Curved coffee table, c. 1970. Burled wood with chrome plated steel. 48" x 27" x 15.25". *Courtesy of Wright.*

Metal with Lacquer 600

This series (1976) featured lacquer with wood in the middle. A popular design in the line was a cylinder table with a glass top, which appeared to float out of it. (As with all his designs, Evans always indicated detailed instructions about the shape and thickness for a glass piece.) The legs for the tables were molded from high-density foam.

Directional catalog page, 1976. *Courtesy of Dorsey Reading.*

Directional catalog page, 1976. *Courtesy of Dorsey Reading.*

Collection 77

Introduced in 1977 and known as "Collection 77," this line was made with poured concrete and stainless steel, and usually covered in leather. One of the larger tables in the series had a concrete base weighing 600 pounds covered in leather, with the legs set in the table corners covered in suede. The "Collection 77" Executive Desk had concrete covered with stainless steel with a stainless steel top with leather and dovetail drawer pulls. Buffets, cabinets, and wall units in the line were also covered in leather.

Collection 77 Directional catalog page, 1977. *Courtesy of Dorsey Reading.*

Brushed Nickel, Satin Chrome Tables 800

In this 1973-1978 series, Evans was running out of ideas and decided to reintroduce polished metal finishes for a group of designs he liked from the past. This included finishes with stainless steel and walnut burl, black lacquer and polished chrome, and cabinet fronts with verdigris copper. Table legs in the series were often curved on the inside and gave the appearance of pushing through to the surface of the tabletop. Placing a matching piece of metal or wood on the corner tops of the table created the effect.

PE-809 Dining table in diagonal marquetry with triangular stainless steel legs – 84w 44d 29h with two 15" leaves. Extends to 114". Shown with **6309** chair –21w 28½d 33½w.

(Below) **PE-875** Shirred bed – King size: 106 long 83½ wide 30 high.
Queen size: 106 long 65½ wide 30 high.
PE-830 Night tables for bed (specify L or R) 30w 10d 23h.
PE-883 Multi-level mirror – 51w 15d 68h.
Mirror/shelf group – shown: polished and brushed chrome.
Night tables – shown: white lacquer. Available in all other finishes.

PE-742 Backgammon table– 39w 28½d 29h. Shown: Satin chrome with suede. Spun aluminum and bronze playing pieces.

PE-826 Chess table – 32w 32d 29h. Shown: Polished chrome frame with leather playing surface. Available in all other finishes.
PE-874 Upholstered game chair – 21w 27d 34h.

PE-825 Game table – 35w 35d 29h. Shown: English oak with polished chrome legs. Available in all other finishes. Shown with **U-160** dining chair.

Directional catalog page, 1978.
Courtesy of Dorsey Reading.

900

Very few pieces were produced for the 900 Series. It was not a complete line and fewer designs were introduced than the usual thirty pieces Evans did for previous lines. It may be considered the beginning of the end for Evans. The series was not formally developed because of changes with Directional, which eventually led to the end of Evans relationship with the company.

1000

Series 1000 was based on a new product at the time called alucobond. Evans was asked by the manufacturer to experiment with the material in the design of furniture. Alucobond has two thin layers of aluminum with a thin layer of rubber-like material in between the aluminum. It could round corners and stay in one piece. Doors on a cabinet could be cut from the same continuous piece of material. Alucobond did not last long, especially at lower temperatures when the rubber became brittle and would break or tear. The solution for reducing stress on the bent corners of the alucobond was to cut a "v" groove on the aluminum surface and place a hinge on the cut side so it could be attached to a cabinet. This kept the exterior side of the surface smooth. The alucobond could then open and close like a door. Evans used the material for radiator covers and routed it for air to circulate. It was sometimes covered with stainless steel. The manufacturer provided Evans with the material for about a year. Since it was too easily damaged, Evans stopped using it. Directional liked the line but it never went into production, so fewer than fifty pieces were produced. In 1981 Evans removed the alucobond pieces from the Directional showroom and placed them in his own showroom in New York City. Today alucobond is often used for architectural paneling.

Cabinet with two doors, c. 1980. Alucobond, burled walnut. 30" x 39.5" x 18". *Courtesy of Rago Arts and Auction Center.*

Commissions

Paul Evans received many of his first commissions from people going to the Bucks County Playhouse in New Hope in the early 1960s. The showroom Evans and Powell shared was near the Playhouse. It was common in the summer months for people from New York and Philadelphia to come into the showroom before and after a play.

One of the earliest commissions was in 1959 for Shari Lewis, the children's television personality. Several custom pieces, including a metal screen, wall collage, and cabinets, were made for her apartment on Riverside Drive in New York City. Evans also made pieces for a second apartment in the same building, before Lewis's move to California.

Writer Paddy Chayefsky was another client and the commission involved both Evans and Powell. For Chayefsky's Manhattan apartment, Evans did cabinets, and ceiling lights that were wrapped with rawhide and had ceramic pulls made by New Hope ceramist Warner Jacobsen. Eventually the rawhide dried out from the heat and the lights fell to the floor. The lights were then replaced with a steel rod.

When, in the early 1960s, woodworker George Nakashima was commissioned to renovate the interior of St. Martin's Church in New Hope, Pennsylvania, he approached Paul Evans and Phillip Lloyd Powell for ideas. The two designers then created a set of twelve to fifteen steel and brass, concave saucer-shaped candleholders for Nakashima.

Evans most public commission was in 1963 for the new Hilton Hotel on Avenue of the Americas in New York City. Evans received the commission through America House, which offered a service that put architects and decorators in contact with craftsmen.

For its interior public spaces, the Hilton displayed artwork by Leonard Baskin, Ben Shahn, Stuart Davis, Lee Krasner, Larry Rivers, and others. Commissions such as Evans's were part of the hotel's design to highlight various types of art. For the commission Evans created *Mercury Wings*, four sculptures made with a steel armature, each shaped into an 8-foot long wing. The top, outer portion of each wing was covered in welded metal patchwork. The inside of each wing was curved to the shape of the steel to show the body of a bird's wing. The ends of the wings were gold-leafed and mounted in pairs high on the wall near the hotel's Mercury Ballroom.

John Crosby, whose company Thiokol Corp., supplied jet fuel to NASA in the 1960s, commissioned Evans in 1959 to furnish each room in his two-story house in Yardley, Pennsylvania, with studio furniture. Powell was also involved with the commission and made carved walnut walls for the house. It was one of their first commissions together. In addition to the furniture, Evans made verdigris copper pieces, wall covers, and loop screens for radiator covers. During this time, Evans and Powell also worked on a residential commission for Ralph Roberts, founder of Comcast.

For the New York City apartment of Wayne Parrish, the publisher of American Aviation Publications, Evans made two pieces: an 8-foot sculptured front cabinet and an elaborate water fountain made with a 5-foot round ball with water running over the surface of the sculpture. The exterior of the sculpture was a patchwork of copper attached to a steel armature.

Sam Holtzman who operated the Baltimore Luggage Co., makers of Amelia Earhart luggage, bought several of Evans's sculptures and was one of the few clients to buy directly off the showroom floor instead of placing the usual custom order. Each year Holtzman added to his collection of Evans sculptures.

Although Evans did not produce many store fixtures, he was asked by Baltimore friend, Jimmy Hamilton, to make jewelry showcases for his Goldsmith Jewelry Store. The showcases were done with leather interiors, burl and ash exteriors, and glass tops and doors.

In 1972, shortly after having his first heart attack, Evans began work on a commission for Sears and Roebuck, for the company's regional corporate office in St. Davids, outside Philadelphia. For the commission, Evans made a pair of 14-foot by 40-foot high stair-towers set at an angle with eight to ten faceted bronze panels. The Sears commission was part of a three-year relationship, which included Evans's design of a copper, bronze, and pewter patchwork reception desk made with a slate top. The Sears building was later torn down.

Through various contacts, a decorator, whose client was Prince Binder Fisal of the Saudi Royal Family, approached Evans. In 1974 Evans traveled to Saudi Arabia to discuss the details of the $100,000 commission. He did not know specifically what he was expected to do and was having a challenging time coming up with a design. When Evans returned from Saudi Arabia he went to a hobby shop and bought a plastic model of a dirigible. He planned to use it in his presentation to the Prince, recommending that he buy a dirigible and have Evans furnish the interior with his furniture. Evans did several drawings to accompany the presentation. However, Evans received word from the Prince's agent in New York that the Prince changed his mind and was no longer interested in pursuing a commission. Evans never made the presentation, but was able to keep his commission fee.

In 1978, a New York decorator visited the Directional showroom, which resulted in Evans's second commission for a member of the Saudi Royal Family. Evans did a number of pieces for one of the Royal Family's palaces, mostly stock pieces from the Directional catalog. For a princess's bedroom Evans designed a custom bed, a light for the bed, and a ceiling light. The bed was circular, 8 feet in diameter on a 12-foot round platform. A set of cabinets in mirrored brass and chrome formed a semi-circle around the bed. A small, lit panel with eight buttons corresponded to the different functions of each cabinet, giving the princess control for the opening and closing of each cabinet. If the princess pushed button number one, the cabinet at the end of the right side would pop up and reveal the television. Another button rotated the bed for the best viewing of the television. The ceiling light was made with a small clear bulb, three circular brass and chrome pieces, which reflected the rounded polished surfaces of the cabinets. This commission was produced before off-the-shelf electronics existed for this type of use. Dorsey Reading engineered all the mechanisms for the bed and cabinets. The electronics used hydraulic mechanisms with hydraulic fluid to function and were all designed in the Evans workshop. After several years of establishing his own company, Reading received a challenging commission from the Sultan of Brunei based on his work for Evans's commission for the Saudi Royal Family. For the Sultan, Reading created tall motorized, remote-controlled metal cylinders which stored clothing, a television, stereo equipment, and other items.

■ Shari Lewis and Paul Evans in his showroom, 1964. New Hope, Pennsylvania. *Courtesy of Dorsey Reading.*

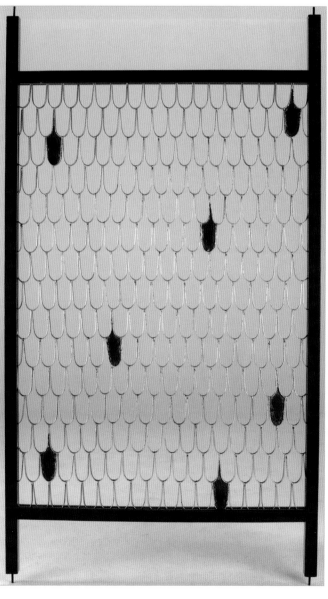

■ A room divider, c. 1959. Part of a larger commission for actress Shari Lewis. Gilded metal loops in a wooden frame in a red washed finish. 88.5" x 51" (frame). *Courtesy of Rago Arts and Auction Center.*

■ Three panel loop screen, 1960. Produced with Phillip Powell for the John Crosby commission. American black walnut, iron, and 22k gold leaf. 49" x 1.5" x 84". *Courtesy of Wright.*

■ Sofa, 1964. Steel and Walnut. Dimensions unknown. *Courtesy private collection.*

■ Wall clock, c. 1970. Part of a larger commission for Evans friend and attorney William Goldman. Gilded metal loopatinated copper, glass. 20" x 7" x 20". *Courtesy of Wright.*

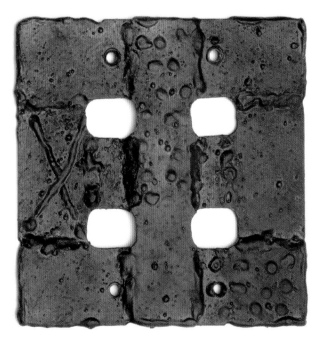

■ Sculpted bronze wall receptacle plate, 1959. John Crosby commission, Yardley, Pennsylvania. 5" x 5". *Courtesy of Rago Arts and Auction Center.*

Conclusion

In the late 1970s, Evans hired consultants, friends of friends, to look for ways to reduce costs and increase production. Evans put these consultants in charge of the factory, even though they did not understand the business. They developed business practices that did not work, which affected their credibility among the craftsmen and factory workers. After three or four months of failure, the consultants either quit or Evans fired them.

The last consultant Evans hired was a businessman from nearby Doyletown, Pennsylvania. He arranged for Evans to borrow a large amount of money from the bank; he promised Evans a lucrative agreement that did not require Evans involvement in the daily operations of the business. This person did not understand the business either, and only looked at the numbers, making statements about meeting the production numbers without knowing how to achieve them. This created problems when it came time to order materials because the same budget for purchasing materials was used for other business expenses. Money often ran out, causing missed or delayed payrolls and, eventually, prohibited the ordering of production materials. This ultimately forced several people to quit, including Dorsey Reading who made the decision to leave in 1982 after working for Evans for 23 years.

Reading set up his own business with a partner and the two of them managed to keep the factory open. Evans was not part of the business and no longer had the finances to secure materials in what was once his own factory. Evans opened his own New York City showroom in 1981, and considered it a great accomplishment. However, he turned his orders over to Reading for production. Reading did most of the research and development when he worked with Evans and continued this approach when he started his new company, Dorsey Reading Studio in 1984. By 1995, Reading decided he had enough of the business and started working as a general contractor, which remains his primary business today.

At the end of his career Evans was designing non-functional, conceptual pieces, intended to attract customers. The market did not respond to the designs and it was clear Evans could not remain in business. The combination of creative pressures, financial issues, and health led to the end of his career. Evans returned to smoking and drinking even after his second heart attack and did nothing about his health. In 1987 he decided to move from New Hope to be with his second wife, Bunny, in Nantucket, Massachusetts. He drove to Nantucket on a Friday and on the next day suffered a third, fatal heart attack. He was 55 years old. Bunny died in 2005.

Today, Evans's sons are craftsmen and run their own businesses. Paul Evans III, formerly known as Ricky, has his own sash and window shop in New England, specializing in historical renovations and restorations. Younger son Keith has a cabinet shop making custom, site-specific furniture. Both sons acknowledge the daily influence their father has on their craft.

Phillip Lloyd Powell continued to operate his own wood shop in Pennsylvania and traveled extensively until his death in 2008 at the age of 89 years old.

Phillip Powell at his home and studio with Dorsey Reading. New Hope, Pennsylvania. 2005. *Courtesy of Wright.*

■ Dining table, c. 1981. Chrome plated steel with lacquered wood (with leaf insert not shown). Made for the Paul Evans New York City showroom. 75" x 58.5" x 29". *Courtesy of Wright.*

■ Detail. Credenza, c. 1981. *Courtesy of Rago Arts and Auction Center.*

■ Credenza with six storage compartments, each with two shelves and two drawers, c. 1981. Black laminate top with polished steel base. Made for the Paul Evans New York City showroom. 36.5" x 118" x 27.5". *Courtesy of Rago Arts and Auction Center.*

133

■ Sculpted cabinet, c. 1972. Bronze. The cat form was a whimsical design for his wife Bunny. 79" x 17" x 17.5". *Courtesy of Wright.*

Wall-hanging cabinet, 1966. Welded and patinated steel with natural cleft slate top. The decorative eye motif was another uncommon figural design. 24" x 48" x 17". *Courtesy of Rago Arts and Auction Center.*

Door. From Paul Evans showroom, 1963. New Hope, Pennsylvania [now installed at a private residence]. Designed and built by Phillip Powell. Carved walnut with metal handle. 32" x 80". *Courtesy of Wright.*

Detail. Paul Evans showroom door, 1963. New Hope, Pennsylvania. *Courtesy of Wright.*

Afterword

Paul Evans is heavy. Damn heavy. For many years Paul Evans furniture was available for not much money, but it was hard to sell and even harder to move. At some point, I told myself, never again. Now Evans pieces achieve six-figure prices and he is the subject of museum shows. The work itself has never changed, but my relationship to it sure has.

Evans is still heavy: the sheer weight and mass of the pieces are key qualities. They create the heroic essence of the work. Always in metal, often topped with stone, the furniture is built to last from sheets of steel. It is furniture of the highest quality.

There is something about Paul Evans that causes extreme reactions. Like the man himself, the furniture is not quiet. A piece of Evans furniture in the room makes a statement. It is big and bold and sometimes ugly. People react to the work – both good and bad. I have experienced both sides of that emotion and have come to see what I first disliked was fueled by the true power that the work holds.

Paul Evans evolved in a stylistic journey that makes him hard to place in the design or craft world. His relationship with craft was complicated to say the least. The heavily welded work is clearly hand-built. The Cityscape series is as well, but the surface, and aesthetics, denies that reading. The truth is more complicated, as Dorsey Reading documents; Evans was the designer and not the maker for most of the furniture, yet the work was almost always finished by hand and done with as much custom variation as the furniture from the nearby Nakashima Studio.

Evans plays with the idea of good taste and good design and walks away from it. Good design meant something very specific at mid-century. There was an almost religious quality to the preaching of good design from Elliot Noyes at the Museum of Modern Art. Safe to say, there is no Paul Evans at MoMA. It is their loss because Evans is part of the story of design in the 20th century. He ignores the boundaries of artist, maker, designer, and good taste and allows his furniture to resonant, to agitate, to be.

— Richard Wright

Chronology

1931	Born in Newtown, Pennsylvania
1949	Graduates from George School Prep
1949	Studies briefly at the Philadelphia Textile School
1949	Apprentices as a metalsmith with his uncle, Ed Truett
1950-52	Attends The School for American Craftsman at Rochester Institute of Technology
1952	Marries Elaine Bebarfald
1952	Wins competition at America House
1952-53	Attends Cranbrook Academy of Art on scholarship
1954	Shows work for the first time at *America House*
1953-55	Works as a traditional craftsman at Sturbridge Village, Massachusetts
1956-66	Collaborates with Phillip Lloyd Powell
1959	Receives Shari Lewis commission
1960	Forms Designer's Incorporated with Philip Lloyd Powell
1960	Establishes long-term collaboration with Dorsey Reading

1961	Shows work with Phillip Lloyd Powell at America House
1961-65	Shows regularly in *America House* catalog
1963	Receives Hilton Hotel, New York City commission for *Mercury Wings* sculpture
1964	Begins designing and manufacturing for Directional Furniture
1970	Sets up a factory in Plumsteadville, Pennsylvania, to produce Directional Furniture
1972	Suffers from first heart attack
1972	Receives Sears commission for stair-tower, St. Davids, Pennsylvania, regional office
1975-76	Height of production for Directional Furniture
1981	Opens own showroom in New York City
1982	Ends relationship with Directional Furniture
1982	Changes at factory cause Dorsey Reading to end working relationship with Evans, leading to the end of formal production.
1987	Dies of heart attack, Nantucket, Massachusetts

Selected Furniture Lines

For Directional (with series number):

11-99 (no 0-10)
Bronze (100)
Chrome (200)
Faceted (300)
Burl and Metal (400)
Curved (500)
Metal with Lacquer (600)
Brushed Stainless Steel and Suede (700). Featured large pieces wrapped in leather or suede with brushed stainless steel, suede and lacquered tops.
Brushed Nickel, Satin Chrome Tables (800)
"900"
"1000"
French 75. Made in 1975 with a sprayed on suede type finish that looked and felt like suede, and was non-repairable when damaged.
Super System. Designed in 1979 – 1980, this was a low budget line distributed by Directional. The line featured upholstered pieces covered in corduroy or gray flannel, and included a corner chair, side chair, chaise lounge and ottoman.
Genesis. Evans designed the Genesis series, a successful line of office furniture for Directional's Contract Division. Desks were made with walnut burl and nickel. Options included all metal, lacquered oak, lacquered or cordovan walnut, and mixed olive ash burl. Most desks were done in burl and featured dovetailed drawers. Directional showed the line along side Evans's other pieces.
Stac-Pak. Another small line for Directional. Designed with a pinstripe finish on formica available on cabinets and tables. All the pieces were custom ordered, not mass produced, making it difficult to compete. The line did not do well; Evans lost money on each piece that was shipped.

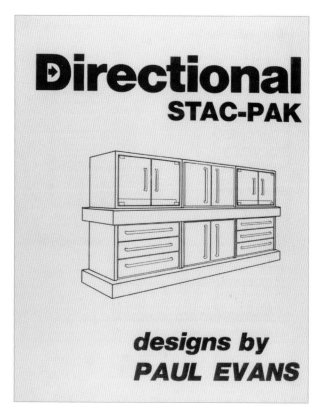

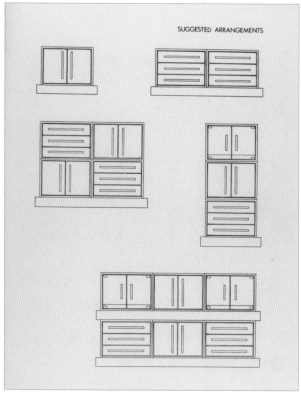

■ Stac-Pak brochure, c. 1981. *Courtesy of Dorsey Reading.*

For Selig Furniture Co

Status – One. For the Selig Furniture Co., from 1981 to 1982, Evans developed, a line of high quality sprayed Plexiglas tabletops for the company's production table bases. In their catalog Selig indicated, "Some pieces are first lacquered, then spackled by hand, so each one is unique." The line included cabinets covered in chrome, and coffee tables with a choice of brass or chrome finish. Evans lost money on the line even though it was relatively quick to produce.

Selig brochure, c. 1981 *Courtesy of Dorsey Reading.*

Selig brochure, c. 1981. *Courtesy of Dorsey Reading.*

Other Designs and Furniture

FORGECRAFT. A line of copper accessories produced for
C.C. Design Inc. from 1963 to 1967.

FORGECRAFT

Patina and texture characterize the Forgecraft Copper Collection, designed by Paul
Evans of New Hope. These handsome,
ruggedly masculine accessories are com-
patible with any decor, contemporary or
traditional.

ECC21 $18.00 PR.

ECC26 $35.00

ECC25 $35.00

ECC27 $35.00

ECC15 $25.00

ECC20 $25.00

ECC28 $35.00

ECC16 $18.00

ECC23 $15.00

ECC17 $18.00

ECC19 $15.00

ECC22 $12.00

ECC18 $18.00

ECC24 $18.00

■ FORGECRAFT brochure, 1963–1967. *Courtesy of Dorsey Reading.*

A FORGECRAFT box, 1963–1967. Paul
Evans for C. C. Design Inc. gift line. Copper
patchwork with cork lined interior and
hinged lid. 3.5" x 14" x 5.5". *Courtesy of Rago
Arts and Auction Center.*

Detail. A Forge Craft box.. 1963–1967. *Courtesy of Rago Arts and Auction Center.*

Corigate. Introduced in late 1978 and produced for about six months, Evans cardboard furniture was marketed to college students. The line included cardboard chairs (covered in Burlap), a lounge chair, a dining table, coffee table, and a cabinet all made with triple-wall cardboard laminated at the Evans factory. Pieces were assembled from cut-out slots and fastened together with two small staples that were pushed in by hand. The furniture was shipped in shrink-wrapped plastic with a cardboard handle.

■ Corigate chairs (one unassembled), 1978. Cardboard covered with burlap. 34" x 18" x 27".
Courtesy of Rago Arts and Auction Center.

Selected Bibliography

Craft Horizons. "Young Americans 1952." (New York, N.Y.). v. 12 (October 1952) p. 38, 39.

Friedman, B. H. *Craft Horizons* (New York, N.Y.). v. 22 (July/August 1963) p. 44.

Hall, Guin. "Craftsman's World–The Workshop–Market for Mementos." *Craft Horizons* (New York, N.Y.). v. 14 (March/April 1954) p. 38-41.

Hammel, Lisa. "Sheet Metal Turns the Ordinary Into Furniture That's Sculpture." *New York Times* (New York, N.Y.), February 23, 1976, p. 33.

Head, Jeffrey. "Heavenly Metal." *Modern Magazine* (New York, N.Y.). p. 40-41.

Interior Design. "Paul Evans on his own." (New York, N.Y.) v. 52 (January 1981) p. 172.

——. "Designer dialogue enlivens ASID/Palm Beach meeting." v. 46 (December 1975) p. 28.

House & Garden. "Up-to-date living in a historic house [Nantucket cottage of Paul and Bunny Evans]." v. 145 (March 1974) p. 96-9.

Interiors. "Sparkle and Shine; Directional Showrooms Inc. Polished Chrome Furniture." (New York, N.Y.) v. 130 (January 1971) p. 42.

——. "America House abets its collections of accessories with new creative furniture created by P. L. Powell and P. Evans." v. 121 (December 1961) p. 142.

Life. "Old Crafts Find New Hands." (New York, N.Y.) v. 61 (July 29, 1966) p. 34.

Loukin, Andrea. "Think tank studio: expanding an already established career as furniture designer, Paul Evans has opened his own showroom." *Interior Design* (New York, N.Y.) v. 52 (March 1981) p. 240-1.

Merrill, Todd, and Julie Iovine. *Modern Americana: Studio Furniture From High Craft to High Glam.* (New York, NY: Rizzoli International Publications, 2008).

New York Times. "Craftsman Shows His Hand." (New York, N.Y.). October 11, 1961, p. 55.

——. "New Beverage Accessories by an English and an American Craftsman." March 11, 1954, p. 24.

Interviews

Dorsey Reading, telephone interview by Jeffrey Head, March 20, 2005.

Dorsey Reading, interview by Jeffrey Head, April 1-2 and August 26-27 2005. Erwinna, Pennsylvania.

Ricky Evans (Paul Evans III.), telephone interview by Jeffrey Head, May 3, 2005.

Keith Evans, telephone interview by Jeffrey Head, May 12, 2005.

Elaine Evans, telephone interview by Jeffrey Head, May 23, 2005.

Phil Powell, telephone interview by Jeffrey Head, July 28, 2005.

Credits and Acknowledgments

I am thankful for the generous support and involvement of many people who made this book possible, all of whom share in their admiration of Paul Evans, for his ability to create a truly unique aesthetic. Dorsey Reading was an invaluable resource. I am most grateful to him. His nearly life-long connection to Paul Evans made it possible for me to appreciate the Evans legacy in a more meaningful way. Dorsey openly shared stories about Evans and offered access to his extensive personal archive. If there is an engaging matter-of-factness to the book, it is a reflection of Dorsey's character.

This book was initiated years ago during discussions with Richard Wright. While it may appear to be self-serving for someone in Richard's position to facilitate the use of documentation and photography, Richard placed greater value on the intrinsic quality of Evans's work. I benefited from Richard's interest in simply wanting to increase people's awareness of Evans's contributions to 20th century design. Exceptional photography by Brian Franczyk and Thea Dickman reinforced that perspective. For those already familiar with Evans, many of the wonderful images you have not seen before are Brian's and Thea's.

Timely support and encouragement came from Todd Merrill. Thank you for your insight and advice. It appears throughout the book. Thanks also to Bella Neyman.

I had enjoyable conversations with Phil Powell, Elaine Evans, Keith Evans, and Ricky Evans. I felt honored by their willingness to talk with me.

Thanks also to Adriana Kertzer, Jennifer Mahanay at Wright, David Rago, Miriam Tucker, and Anthony Barnes at Rago Arts & Auction Center. Everyone at Rago was especially helpful and gave me more than I asked for throughout the process. Becky Simmons at the Rochester Institute of Technology, Erin McAndrew at Christie's, James Zemaitis and Megan Whippen at Sotheby's, Peter Gleeson, Steve Aldana and Objects USA, and my friend Lawrence Converso. Special thanks to Catherine Gowen for your questions and interest while I was in the midst of it. You helped me focus.

Ultimate thanks to Nancy Schiffer and Peter Schiffer. Nancy, you immediately, intuitively understood the nature of what I hoped for with the book. I kept our first conversation in mind and it always made me feel good...and still does. I appreciate your personal attention in wanting to see the book as we envisioned it. Thank you to Senior Editor Douglas Congdon-Martin and everyone at Schiffer.